D1565118

BODY LANGUAGE FOR WOMEN

BODY LANGUAGE FOR WOMEN

Learn to Read People Instantly and Increase Your Influence

DR. DONNA VAN NATTEN
Foreword by Robin Dreeke

Skyhorse Publishing

Skyhorse Publishing books may be purchased in bulk at special discounts for sales promotion, corporate gifts, fund-raising, or educational purposes. Special editions can also be created to specifications. For details, contact the Special Sales Department, Skyhorse Publishing, 307 West 36th Street, 11th Floor, New York, NY 10018 or info@skyhorsepublishing.com.

Skyhorse® and Skyhorse Publishing® are registered trademarks of Skyhorse Publishing, Inc.®, a Delaware corporation.

Visit our website at www.skyhorsepublishing.com.

10 9 8 7 6 5 4 3 2 1

Library of Congress Cataloging-in-Publication Data is available on file.

Cover design by Tom Lau
Cover photo credits: Getty Images

Print ISBN: 978-1-5107-5121-7
Ebook ISBN: 978-1-5107-5123-1

Printed in the United States of America

Table of Contents

Foreword   ix

Chapter 1: What You are Saying with Your Body   1
    Communication Creatures   2
    Talking the Terms   10
    The "I" in Image   12
    Express Yourself   19
    I Feel What I Feel   22
    Cradle to Coffin Nonverbal Communication   26
    Media Mayhem   30

Chapter 2: How to Read Other
        Women's Body Language   35
    Hand it to Her   41
    Can You Read my Body?   43
    In Sync: The Relationship, not the Band   46
    Palpable Peer Power   48
    Color and Culture Caveats   53
    Emotion Potion   60

Chapter 3: Mastering Men's Body Language   65
    When I Grow Up, I Want to Be   67
    Man in the Mirror   71

Boys Will be Boys; Some Men Will be Menacing   75
Catcalls and Compliments   79
Bodies, Brains, and Behaviors   85
Stress and the Sexes   88

Chapter 4: Family and Friends' Body Language   91
Pinky Promises   97
So Much Commotion Over Our Emotions   100
Planting the Seeds   104
You've Got a Friend in Me   107
Confidants in My Corner   113

Chapter 5: The Powerful Body Language for Love   118
You Make Me Feel Alright   121
Come-hither Look   127
Tall, Dark, and Handsome?   131
Rearing its Ugly Head   135
Touch and Go   140

Chapter 6: Influence is More than Impact   146
Here a Little, There a Little   149
Pearly Whites   155
Fibbers, Facts, and Falsehoods   159
Belly Laugh   165
You Go, Girl . . . and Boy   170

Ponderings   176
Bibliography   183
Acknowledgments   193

Foreword

Imagine a world where everyone has the limitless ability to achieve their dreams. A world with abundant resources, where struggle and strife dissipate as fast as a mere thought. Many think that this majestic existence is achieved through the accumulation of material possessions and wealth. However, self-aware and emotionally intelligent individuals who are the inspirational leaders in all walks of life know the secret—building healthy and happy relationships. Almost anyone can be taught a skill, but it is those who can form relationships that can bring their skills, expertise, and ideas to the world. Not just for their own success and prosperity, but also for the good of others.

Strong, healthy relationships are the key to success in every aspect of life. We are genetically and biologically "coded" to act in terms of safety, security, and prosperity for ourselves and our families. As well, we all have insecurities. Our insecurities are founded in the fear of not being accepted and valued by those around us. This book provides a deep understanding of these doubts and the tools that allow us to capitalize on our strengths and overcome these challenges.

As the retired Chief of the FBI Counterintelligence Behavioral Analysis Program, and an author of books on the subject of trust, my experience has taught me that decoding nonverbal behavior, building confident expectations, and inspiring healthy relationships is the key to prosperity. Donna's book provides you with the tools to help you learn these skills. Donna not only exudes high energy, commitment, and expertise to her craft, but she adds a unique view, or "context," that many experts overlook. Donna's book not only focusses on the nonverbal behavior of women, but also their self-image. Self-image is a critical component for understanding and communicating effectively with anyone.

This book is perfect for women who want to be able to understand more deeply how self-image begins from childhood experiences, including culture and social media impact. The challenges that many women face regarding their own self-image and how this impacts their daily interactions and communication are illuminating. The book is a handy tool to help enhance all relationships—whether personal or professional.

This is not a typical book about nonverbal behavior, but it is a deep look inside the minds of women attempting to navigate our complicated world of relationships while, at the same time, battling themselves and their own self-images. Donna is a master at looking at nonverbal behavior and gives us insight into how to assess others to determine their needs, wants, desires, intentions, and fears. Once you understand that and you establish trust, healthy, strong relationships quickly follow.

People want to be appreciated, they want to be cared for, loved, trusted, and respected, but they also want to be understood. If you master the skills to achieve that, you truly become exceptional. You become one of those people we read about who is well-respected, well-liked, and sought after. That is the power of interpreting nonverbal behavior for the purpose of building relationships, as Donna articulates.

Donna's lifetime of study and practical experience as a coach, teacher, trainer, and mentor has provided her the tools, strategies, and secrets to working with others and establishing trust. These skills, practiced by a knowledgeable few in high-stakes situations, will certainly work for you in your daily life. Written in a very practical style, full of examples and anecdotes, *Body Language for Women* is a book for anyone who is interested in understanding themselves—and, more importantly, understanding others.

The content illuminates the reader in areas that some term the "elusive obvious." The information and concepts make so much sense; yet, they have never been articulated in such an easy and logical way that it's almost embarrassing you didn't think of it before. Whatever your role in this world, this book will provide you with the deeper understanding and insight you need to create stronger and healthier relationships in all aspects of your life.

—Robin Dreeke
FBI Special Agent (Retired)
Author of *The Code of Trust* and *Sizing People Up*

CHAPTER 1

What You are Saying with Your Body

We, as women, spend countless hours trying to perfect our physical bodies and mental mindsets. Beyond this, we must also know what subtle, unconscious, and powerful messages our bodies send and receive.

The advice we always hear is, "Don't judge a book by its cover." And yet, we do.

Let's face it: we like to think that how we carry ourselves, look, and behave are secondary to how smart we are, who we know, and our job titles. Some even claim that they "just don't care what other people think" about them. On the contrary, all of the research on the subject of people, relationships, and communication says that presentation does matter. And we do judge each other based on a set of specific human behavior characteristics. Even the fact that you are reading this book says that you do care and believe that these traits matter.

This is not necessarily a bad thing, as appearance characteristics give us a lot of information about other people. Their clothing style, how they groom their hair, their smell, and other appearance-based traits all provide us with valuable information. Much of non-verbal communication operates "automatically and often outside of awareness," according to the experts. But the complex intersections of gender, culture, biology, situation, and individual means that our communication is both complex and often predictable. As well, "appearance can also be strategically modified to create desired impressions" (Patterson, 2017).

Nonverbal communication "sparkles and inspires," per Friedman's 2019 extensive review of the literature on this important field of study. He notes that "basic emotions theory" has a wide range of components crossing psychology, language, culture, social conditions, and emotions. Specifically, "behavioral ecology" depends on nonverbal cues in social situations. Basically, our navigation of our world relies on interpreting body language.

COMMUNICATION CREATURES

In 1872, Charles Darwin wrote about the expression of emotions in humans and in animals. Darwin understood creatures, their social weaving, and how they communicated through emotions. and nonverbal actions. Modern theorists converge on his work and now look at nonverbal communication in terms of a "functional" approach. As a result, we think about what we are doing. Three major shifts of thought now focus on:

1. Cognitive abilities tied to emotions: our thoughts and our feelings are closely intertwined.
2. Abstract traits to concrete abilities: our thoughts turn into actions.
3. Inferred states to processes: our deductive thoughts generate actual operations.

Nonverbal communication has the power to influence and persuade. By looking at people in groups (relational impression model), we emit and receive information about other people. We also make impressions on others. In the field of the social psychology of influence, the evidence is rich, and we are well-served to dip into this bank of knowledge.

Often, we are not even aware that we use body language. Even so, we continuously receive and interpret others' body language. Specifically, we primarily use nonverbal communication— which includes *tone of voice* (nonverbal-vocal) and *body movements* (nonverbal-nonvocal). As visual creatures, we continually use our sight to look at ourselves and our world. In addition, our bodies' movements help us deliver and receive information.

"Whenever the behavior of one individual (the sender) influences the behavior of another individual (the receiver)" this constitutes communication (Mandal, 2014). Mandal writes that nonverbal behaviors include:

- Everything from facial expressions and gestures to fashion and status symbol.
- From dance and drama to music and mime.
- From flow of affect to flow of traffic.
- From the territoriality of animals to the protocol of diplomats.
- From the sensitivity of violence to the mindlessness of topless dancers.

Traffic to topless dancers? That's pretty substantial—and broad. We don't often think about how our actions communicate. We usually only cite our verbal messages when we are asked to define "communication." However, this is not the case. Long before we used the spoken language, we communicated using signs, symbols, our bodies, and other nonverbals. Clear evidence of this is the fact that infants "talk" to us though they have no knowledge of English or any other language. But they do have body language and nonverbals that they understand and master early on. A cry. A gasp. A reach for the hand. A smile. A coo. A stretch.

Even a surprised expression. Yes, babies talk and seek our attention, and we give it to them. A key part of nonverbal communication is being intentional with the signals we send and receive through our senses. In particular, our basic visual (see), auditory/acoustic (hear),

Getty Images

tactile (touch), and olfactory (smell) senses. Of course, how other people interpret various nonverbal signals through their own senses varies greatly based on a host of conditions. For example, time and situation help us to interpret nonverbal signals even though they are not technically a part of body language. As well, we may smell a pleasant odor and immediately recall a good memory. Though it may have happened decades ago, we instantaneously associate it with feelings, people, and situations.

To cultivate Darwin's early work, researchers such as Paul Ekman, Desmond Morris, David Matsumoto, Roger Axtell, and others focus on classifying the thousands of pieces of nonverbal communication and body language. For example, the work of Meadors and Murray (2014) breaks down body language into three elements with specific meanings:

1. *Illustrators*: These usually enhance what is being said— like a nod of the head to emphasize the spoken word.
2. *Emotional expressions*: These expressions typically display how someone is feeling and are often seen in facial expressions. For example, a downturned mouth

with slumped body posture may indicate a person's sadness. Some emotional expressions are globally understood, such as smiles.

3. *Manipulators*: These are exhibited when one part of our body manipulates another part of our body—like self-hugging or stroking. Manipulators usually involve touching our body, or directly interacting with another person (interpersonal interaction). We may shift our body to sit further away from someone we don't enjoy being near. It might be subtle and, at times, unconscious.

Let's focus more on manipulators and body language. A quick look at this photo of a woman on the couch should tell you something about her . . . and it's not good. By looking more closely at the woman, you are able to figure out other things about her and how she is communicating with her body. Why is one hand on her stomach and the other on her forehead? What about her closed eyes? Why is she lying down? These questions, based on what we "see," provide us with information about her. The following

Getty Images

list may help us determine how others "act" to communicate their inner thoughts and feelings.

These visible displays of body language include specific actions:

A. "Shielding actions": Face touching (eyes, mouth, nose, etc.) may signal that we want to reduce sensory input.

B. "Cleaning actions": Hair and grooming attention may improve our physical appearance—or may help to build a relationship when we groom or preen someone else.

C. "Self-intimacies": Holding or stroking the body serves as a means to comfort or console ourselves.

The quality of our nonverbal physical movements are outward displays of our emotional (internal) state. We may be feeling something and, without really thinking about it, we display that feeling through our body language. For the most part, we can control these if we are acting intentionally. However, there are numerous times when our bodies "call us out" in truth. For example, you are feeling terrible about something and when someone asks, you tell this person that you are "fine." But then, your eyes shift down and tears begin to slide down your cheeks. You are far from "fine." Your body language betrayed your words and we know the truth.

Remember, though, that no single nonverbal characteristic is linked to a specific emotion. It's more complex. Yet, we know that emotion-related movements are tied to specific emotions. Dynamic changes in the body may include:

1. Body shifts.
2. How we use space.
3. How we adjust our bodies to our environment or situation.

The amount of effort it takes to physically communicate through the movement of our bodies is also involved. Crane and Gross's

(2013) chart of body movements intimately linked to specific basic emotions is enlightening.

	Anger	Joy	Sadness	Contentment	Neutral
Torso	Expanded, stretched, growing	Expanded, stretched, growing	Contracted, shrinking, bowed	Expanded, stretched, growing	Expanded, stretched, growing
Limb	Moves away from body, expanded	Moves away from body, expanded	Moves close to body, contracted	Neither expanded nor contracted	Neither expanded nor contracted
Space (focused or wandering)	Focused, direct	Focused, direct	Wandering, indirect	Focused, direct	Neither direct nor indirect
Energy (forceful or light)	Forceful, powerful	Forceful, powerful	Light, delicate	Neither forceful nor light	Light, delicate
Time (sustained or quick)	Quick, hurried	Quick, hurried	Sustained, slow	Sustained, slow	Sustained, slow
Flow (relaxed or tense)	Tense, controlled	Neither relaxed nor tense	Relaxed, uncontrolled	Relaxed, uncontrolled	Relaxed, uncontrolled

It's thought-provoking that anger and joy share a lot of similarity in body movement or presentation. And, not surprisingly, feelings of contentment and neutrality are comparable. Sadness, as most of us know, is uniquely recognizable with its own set of body displays. Think about how "still" your body is when you are sad. Or, how "quick and tense" you feel when angered. Most of can read the nonverbal displays of anger, joy, sadness, or contentment; few, if any, words are required.

We tend to gesture more when we are describing or acting out a physical activity or motion. For example, the way we move our bodies to show someone how to wrap a package versus explaining a written report to someone. We "gesture [more] when we express thoughts that involve simulations of action" (Hostetter and Alibali, 2010). In terms of communication, this is important to know for how we reinforce our verbal message or communicate with someone only using our bodies.

A specific set of displays, called representational gestures, are manual movements of our bodies, especially when we use our hands and arms to describe something. Interestingly, these are evident in both sighted and blind people.

Also, how we use space to communicate is critical for ensuring that our unspoken intentions are accurate. Public, social, personal, and intimate spaces are important for communicating and can evoke both positive and negative feelings. Don't invade someone's

Getty Images

space and actually expect that everything is okay just because that person kept quiet. We call this "creeping," harassment, or in some cases, stalking. A quick glance at this photo tells us that he is being inappropriate by standing too close to her.

The power of space in nonverbal communication conveys a lot about the sender, situation, and receiver. Hall (1963) coined "proxemics" as important to nonverbal communication in terms of space and interpersonal communication. The use of space "talks" about the situation and how people act within it.

Hall's breakdown of space shows which of these different spaces are used based on the nature of the relationship between individuals. Specifically:

Intimate space: Touching, whispering, and holding between very close family and friends. This space is also reserved for sexual intimacy. This distance is typically between one inch and eighteen inches, depending on the person and situation.

Personal space: Reserved for good friends and family members with an established relationship. We even call this our "personal space" as we hold out our arms to demonstrate. Personal distance is usually between one and a half feet and up to four feet.

Social space: As its name infers, this distance is reserved for social situations. Perhaps you are having a conversation with a colleague or sales associate. Group discussions typically use this type of space by spreading our bodies around a large table. This distance ranges from four to twelve feet depending on social dynamics.

Public space: Situations in which we don't know each other or participate in large audience, group, or stranger activities, this space retains a large distance between strangers. At a minimum, this space requires at least twelve feet of distance and is based on the fact that we are not comfortable with the other person or people surrounding us.

Wherever we go, our space accompanies us and lets others know something about us. Too often, though, people invade our space, both intentionally and accidentally, and we are set on high alert. This is simple biology. The closer someone gets to us, the safer we must feel to allow them to remain physically close to us—our lives may depend on it. Consider how you feel walking across a dark parking lot by yourself at night. Your gait is quicker. Your eyes dart back and forth scanning the parking lot. Your body leans forward. And your hands and arms clutch your bag or keys. No one should come near you—especially a male. This space and our safety are critical. This powerful nonverbal expression is clearly displayed through our body language.

TALKING THE TERMS

We hear "body language" and "nonverbal communication" and instantly understand what these mean in terms of communication and engaging with another person. Yet, clarification of the two terms is warranted so that we can better understand our own bodies and how we engage with others. Body language as defined by the Merriam Webster dictionary includes, "the gestures, movements, and mannerisms by which a person or animal communicates with others." Nonverbal communication is defined as, "gestures, facial expressions, and body positions (known collectively as 'body language'), as well as unspoken understandings and presuppositions, and cultural and environmental conditions that may affect any encounter between people."

Specific to nonverbal communication, more than just the body in involved. Patterson's (2017) extensive work on nonverbal communication offers the following specific characteristics.

1. The nonverbal channel is always "on" in social settings. Even when people don't speak, we watch and "read" their body movements and vocal sounds. Just their physical presence enables us to judge others and better understand them.
2. Nonverbals are fast. Both sending and receiving signals can happen at the same time. And we quickly respond or adjust. We constantly make "subtle adjustments to other people" in different settings based on numerous factors.

3. Most of our nonverbal messages happen without much thought. It's rather automatic and we are not aware of these signals. Because we constantly send and receive nonverbal cues without really thinking about it, our brains aren't burdened. Rather, we are "cognitively efficient."

4. Most nonverbal communication has a set of patterns. From eye contact toward someone we like to body shifting away from something we don't like, this never-ending "dance" helps us control ourselves when engaging with others.

Additionally, nonverbal communication includes the use of time and how we control our physical environment. Should I sit or stand? And, if I sit, which chair should I pick? Should I hold my bag in front of my body? Subconsciously, we make hundreds of decisions every day about how we maneuver ourselves when around other people. "Nonverbal" may be considered the generic term for which many specific non-verbalized elements exist, including body language.

A large part of this is how our entire bodies, from head to toe, communicate via nonverbal clues and cues. The emphasis on facial expression, gestures, body positions, and physical movements of our bodies is a part of body language. Touch (haptics), space (proxemics), breathing, vocal (tone of voice), and subtle behavioral cues also add to our understanding of body language. This is a complex language to learn with countless nuances.

As we seek to understand the language of the body, we evaluate "wordless signals" and cues like facial gestures, body postures, and eye contact. Simultaneously, we take in and evaluate dozens of nonverbal cues to help us understand each other. We know that posture is a "particularly powerful tool in both expressing and recognizing emotion" (Kana and Travers, 2012).

In the spirit of how we communicate, the overarching umbrella of body language and nonverbal communication are intimately intertwined. The two mimic each other, and we communicate through all channels while making judgements of others and ourselves. It's a complex interplay. We are constantly subjected to body actions and nonverbal cues because we live in societies and are social beings. According to Brook and Servatka (2016), "Almost two-thirds of the meaning of a social encounter is derived from nonverbal cues . . . and, the use of wordless signals and cues play a prominent role in communication."

Along these lines, Albert Mehrabian's well-known "7-38-55 Rule" suggests that seven percent of our communication is based on our words, thirty-eight percent comes from our tone of voice, and fifty-five percent of our message is based on our body language. While some challenge these numbers, countless studies by brilliant researchers confirm (and continue to reaffirm) that the overwhelming majority of how we communicate comes from our nonverbal channels—our bodies and our vocals, but not necessarily our words, tell the story of us.

Mehrabian remains a pioneer in the field and his contributions are impressive. As we look at the history of nonverbal communication and body language, think about the imprint we make—particularly as women in today's evolving world. More women are entering politics. Women now outnumber men in college. Worldwide, our earth is half female and half male.

THE "I" IN IMAGE

"Perceived appearance is the single strongest predictor of global self-esteem among young adults," according to Balcetis et al. (2013). You may not like that finding, but it's a tough one to challenge. Perceptions are powerful. And, regardless of how you feel about appearance and judgment based on individual physicality, many people determine their self-worth based on how they believe other people will judge them. The ways that we communicate with our bodies has a lot to do with how we feel about our bodies.

For women in one study who reported "moderate body image" concerns about their shape/weight, Becker and team (2017) note that these women experience the following:

- 67% feel critical about themselves.
- 43% are upset.
- 41% feel ashamed.
- 43% experience guilt.
- 41% worry.
- 33% feel like a failure.

One in four (24 percent) also state that their negative body image interferes with enjoying life and negatively impacts their relationships.

As you look at these numbers, I don't believe you are surprised. The fact that more than half or almost half of us have these negative feelings about ourselves and our body image is not unexpected. It comes out through our nonverbals and our internal self-image and self-esteem.

Self-esteem is influenced by knowing the ideal standards for beauty. Women with lower self-esteem fixate on their physical appearance. And, sadly, experts continue to link self-esteem issues to problems with mental health, depression, anxiety, and feelings of unhappiness.

Specific emotions are also correlated with our body image and self-esteem. Women, in particular, who feel disappointed with how they look, often feel ashamed. Unhappiness often stems from perception of one's size—with most women seeking to be thinner. When we focus on the body instead of the personality, we question our self-worth. And our body language will often reveal our negative feelings of worth through slumped shoulders, downturned eyes, facial micro expressions, and similar nonverbals.

Self-esteem can change based on situations throughout the day; however, chronically low self-esteem negatively impacts physical and mental well-being. One 1997 study found that "young women today believe that 'good looks' rather than 'good works' serve as a marker for success" (Balcetis et al.). The need to be validated solely based on our physical appearance is real and dangerous. The data is alarming.

The trio of perceived, ideal, and others' views has significant ramifications for women's body image and self-esteem. Even though both genders worry about their weight and image, dissatisfaction and negative feelings are much more common in both girls and women. Stephens, Hill, and Hanson (1994) note that one-third to half of women with healthy weight perceive themselves as "too heavy" compared to only one-fourth of normal-weight men who consider themselves to be overweight. The sad reality is that these women experience decreased satisfaction with their bodies, lower self-esteem, and lower well-being compared to men who are a healthy weight.

In America, the majority of women find dissatisfaction with their bodies. "I'm so fat" is a common female complaint (Gillen and Lefkowitz, 2011). Balcetis et al. (2013) say that American women's dissatisfaction with their bodies has doubled in the last thirty years. While being thin has been considered ideal historically, current research suggests that women may be shifting the definition of "ideal thin" to an athletic body type ideal, which looks like thinness accompanied by muscle tone. Watson, et al. (2019) looked at three female body types: thin, athletic (muscular and thin), and hyper-muscular (extremely muscular and moderately thin). The results are interesting. Overall, researchers suggest that women don't want to be muscular, but desire their bodies to either be thinner or thinner and toned.

As a whole, we tend to be poor judges of our body size. Most women believe they are larger than their actual size. In America, the female ideal body is lean. For men, the ideal figure is muscular and lean. However, achieving the "ideal" is nearly impossible, and the pursuit of that ideal can have grave consequences on the body, mind, and spirit.

"When people focus on the physical aspects of a person (e.g., physical appearance, body shape, clothing), they are less likely to focus on that person's more internal, psychological states" (Guyer et al., 2019). How people live their lives and feel about themselves are impacted through unhealthy eating, depression, smoking, physical activity, and anxiety.

Stephens, Hill, and Hanson's (1994) work adds to the stereotype that "physically unattractive, overweight individuals are expected to be less intelligent, popular, or outgoing than those who are slimmer." Others who study this topic find that heavy persons are often labeled as "lonely, dependent, and greedy for affection." This supposed "character flaw" is associated with laziness and self-indulgence. Basically, "fat is seen as self-induced." Really? We know that this is far from the truth. I don't know a single person who hopes to gain weight and is disappointed if the scale betrays her. Weight is much more complicated than a simple choice. And, sadly, this starts in childhood.

"The majority of women are dissatisfied with their bodies and when asked about the specific source of body dissatisfaction, most women point to body weight and shape" (Alleva et al., 2014). In

Courtesy of Markus Spiske

Western societies, body weight issues are so common that they have actually been called "a normative discontent" (Webster and Tiggeman, 2003). The desire to be thin or attain the ideal body shape is impossible for many women; yet this belief consumes them. In my opinion, this "normative discontent" is not acceptable.

Heavier women are assigned labels such as less intelligent, less popular, or less outgoing. Basically, their weight proves they have a "character flaw" of self-indulgence. Such body shaming is directly linked to self-esteem, well-being, mental health, eating disorders, sexual dysfunctions, and critical brain performance. And you can imagine how this presents itself through body language and social encounters. It's often not good.

Women may "hate" one or two areas of their bodies, but may be satisfied with other areas. Regardless, negative body image is strongly correlated with numerous self-reported negative behaviors and thoughts like:

- Lower quality of life.
- Increased functional impairment.
- Less physical activity enjoyment.
- Depression or dangerous thoughts.
- Decreased consumption of healthy food.
- Poor sleep.

Fortunately, the opposite holds true; positive body image improves quality of life, including sleeping, physical activity, and healthy eating.

Positive body image is also linked to optimism. A study by Dalley and Vidal (2013) looked at four characteristics of women's body image specific to their body appreciation. Specifically, they measured:

1. Favorable opinions of one's body.
2. Acceptance of an imperfect body.
3. Respect of one's body via healthy behaviors.

4. Protecting the body from unrealistic social media images.

They find that positive body image is associated with a woman's internalized standard of attractiveness. And, with feelings of optimism, fears and negative thoughts can be better managed.

We must be careful of the influence of external factors on our quest for a positive body image as we display ourselves through nonverbal and verbal channels. We know that many mainstream values hurt the way women view their bodies and value themselves. One study focused on women in college finds that more than eighty percent are dissatisfied with their bodies. And, sadly, a staggering seventy-one percent of women over fifty years of age report "dissatisfaction with their weight" (Becker et al., 2017). It seems like aging and time have little to do with our bodies, how we feel about them, and how we communicate our messages to others with them.

When we focus on appearance and assign value to it, we are "seen as less fully human." One study asked women to try on bathing suits and then sweaters while standing in front of dressing room mirrors. These women's own comments on their bodies while wearing swimsuits were consistently focused on body shaming and elicited negative body-related thoughts, both during and long after the experiment was over.

The ideal "thin equals beauty" mindset continues to plague our society and our minds. We are also significantly influenced by the media's fascination with this concept. Our incessant outward monitoring of our body appearance leads to habitual self-objectification. Are we just what we see when we look in the mirror? There are negative consequences with self-objectification including increased anxiety, body shaming, and depression.

A popular example of self-objectification is the fascination with cosmetic surgery—the optional expensive procedures that millions choose to undergo. Cosmetic surgery is often undertaken to modify a person's body in hopes of altering their mind. Cosmetic procedures change body shapes to meet society's "ideal"—with liposuction and

Getty Images

breast augmentation being the top two elective procedures in the US (Overstreet et al., 2010).

Two million people going under the knife every year generates big business opportunities. It's actually a yearly sixteen billion—yes, I said billion—dollar industry with the most popular procedures targeting women. Almost three hundred thousand breast augmentations were performed in 2017 with a cost of roughly $4,000 each. And, according to plasticsurgery.org, 17.1 million cosmetic procedures were performed in 2016. Additionally, modifications to the face hit an all-time high as people sought instant facial improvements.

Dr. Debra Johnson, ASPS President shared,

> While there are more options than ever to rejuvenate the face, a facelift done by a board-certified plastic surgeon can give a dramatic, longer-lasting result, which is why I am not surprised to see facelifts back in the top five most popular cosmetic surgical procedures.

How does that narrative make you feel? I *highly doubt* that reshaping your face is an "improvement"—let alone "instant."

However, perhaps you have just taken a quick glance in the mirror to examine your own face and questioned what a little "nip and tuck" might do for it.

Duan et al.'s (2018) research on nonverbal communication finds that facial expressions are important for understanding another person. We look at the face for nonverbal cues to validate verbal messages and to understand emotions. The face, with all of its expressiveness, is critical for body language and nonverbal communication. Just think about the challenge of reading a face after it has been injected with Botox, which paralyzes some of the very muscles required for many nonverbal expressions. It puzzles us at times—or, at least, amuses us—as we look at overly plumped and pulled faces. According to Dr. David Neal at the University of Southern California (2011), "Human communication can be a very subtle thing. When you eliminate a slice of information—whether by communicating through email and Twitter or by paralyzing your own facial muscles—it can be the difference between successful communication and failure."

On the other hand, social media has adapted to include emoticons (smiley faces), Bitmojis (personalized characters), and avatars (computer generated caricatures) to express nonverbal language beyond the written word. We feel compelled to communicate with our bodies, real or artificial, across all communication channels as a way of expressing our thoughts. More specifically, by cultivating optimistic views of our physical appearance, we change how others view us. Our body language is an outward display of our internal frame of mind.

EXPRESS YOURSELF

Expressions are a part of communication and have a broad range of meanings. Experts cluster our emotions into "emotion families" because various emotions have shared characteristics. The following chart is based on Sauter's (2017) work on types of "positive" emotions and what they have in common.

Type of positive "emotion family"	What the type of "emotion family" means	Specific positive emotions that we understand and see nonverbally
Theory	We change in knowledge or understanding; *new information.*	Amusement, relief, awe, and interest.
Agency	We feel the potential for a *reward.*	Elation and pride.
Prosocial	We feel for *others' well-being.*	Love, compassion, gratitude, admiration.
Savoring	We have a *physical* payoff.	Contentment, sensory pleasure, and sexual desire.

Diving a little deeper into specific "emotion families," Sauter (2017) notes that specific body gestures accompany each positive emotion. When we get new information and/or have physical enjoyment, we use specific nonverbals. This shouldn't surprise you. Think about the last time you were surprised or hugged. Most likely, you expressed nonverbals with your body like a subtle change in your skin or body temperature, a shift in your breathing pattern, and facial expressions to match your emotions. Specific to individuals, new information and physical enjoyment are recognizable in part by the body language we display.

Positive Emotions	Body Language We Display
Amusement (funny)	√ Duchenne smiles (real smiles with crinkled corners of the eyes while smiling). √ Intense smile with open jaws. √ Straight head position. √ Laughter (face and full body).
Relief (unpleasant emotion ends)	√ Sighs. √ Low-intensity smiles followed by mouth opening. √ Eyes closed. √ Head tilting up. √ Hands may move to the pockets. √ Relaxed body position.

(continued on next page)

Positive Emotions	Body Language We Display
Awe (greater than one's self)	√ Widened eyes. √ Forward head movements. √ Open mouth with slightly dropped jaw. √ Raised inner eyebrows. √ Also, we hear inhalations and exhalations. √ Sometimes we get goosebumps.
Interest (wanting to learn more)	√ Open mouth or pressed lips. √ Faster rate of speech and frequency range. √ No facial smiling. √ Open mouth. √ Mild squinting or eyes closed. √ Slightly tilting head to one side.
Contentment (satisfying basic needs)	√ Duchenne smiles (real smiles with crinkled corners of the eyes while smiling). √ Lips pressed together. √ Sighs. √ Relaxed body posture.
Sensory pleasure (enjoying physical stimulus)	√ Tilting head up and away. √ Symmetric arm movements. √ Smiles. √ Eyes closed. √ Mouth open.
Sexual desire (seeking sexual activity)	√ Lip licks. √ Lip bites. √ Lip puckering. √ Flushed skin. √ Body leaning in.

Additionally, when we stand or sit taller, this elicits positive emotions—we just feel better. We also look healthier, and wouldn't our mothers be proud of our posture! Even producing a fake smile helps us feel better internally. Frowning, not surprisingly, does the opposite.

Regardless of how we feel on this inside, our body language tells others about our internal feelings and thoughts. These internal signals and functions of the body, also known as body functionality, include unobservable dimensions like fitness, health, stamina, agility, and strength. It's vital that we "respect the body by attending to its need and engaging in healthy behaviors" in relationship to body image (Alleva et al., 2014).

I FEEL WHAT I FEEL

It's important to monitor our own behavior (self-monitor) as we seek to have our needs and wants met. Those who exhibit high levels of self-monitoring are able to read social situations and fix their own behaviors—they adapt and do it well. I ask, "Are you a social chameleon?" "Do you feel like you fit in?" "Can others relate to you?"

If the answers to these are no, you may have low self-monitoring behaviors. You may struggle with the demands of situations and feel inflexible. Your freeze, flight, or fight response mechanism may kick into high gear. You might even say, "I don't fit in." However, we all experience these challenges to some degree because we are all human beings. Sometimes it is difficult to communicate and "do it right."

Per the literature, without good coping strategies, many will experience mental health issues, including anxiety and depression. For a few, social anxiety disorder (SAD or social phobia) interferes with their daily lives in the sense that these individuals will avoid interpersonal relationships and primarily operate out of a place of fear. Low self-esteem may contribute to SAD which, over time, has devastating effects for sufferers. Our emotional well-being is a massive part of our overall well-being.

Nonverbally, we recognize basic emotions through posture cues and, often, facial expressions. We seek to confirm that others' words match their actions and when the two aren't aligned, we judge their nonverbals as the more authentic communication source. For example, you watch a supposedly confident and smart woman give a speech; however, she frequently bites her lower lip, wrings her hands together, hides behind the podium, and fails to make eye contact. Her body language does not match her words and we are quickly suspicious. Mandal's (2014) work details several types of feelings and how our body language communicates these through behaviors and actions.

How you feel	What you look like to others
Confident	Preen yourself—touch your hair or face. Look at yourself in mirrors and windows. Display large gestures with your arms and hands. Seek to be the center of attention. Stand or sit with a straight back. Self-assured big smiles. Plenty of eye contact. Good hygiene.
Arrogant	Head tilted back with chin elevated. Display more physical distance. Quit listening and perhaps turning the head away. May make more sexually suggestive movements and postures.
Insecure	May chew on fingers or objects. Eye contact not consistent. Self-deprecating humor. Quiet and courteous behaviors. Body posture may be closed—hugging self. Cross body actions (with arms or legs crossing each other). Hiding part of the body behind an object (table, desk, podium, etc.).
Embarrassed	Avoid eye contact. Shake your head. Turn away. Flushed skin. Nervous laughter.
Fearful	Wide-open eyes while looking around. Freeze your body. Clutch your hands together. Grab other people. Heavy breathing or holding breath. Rigid body. Lick your lips.
Resentment	Cross your arms with a stiff body. Whisper. Cover your mouth with your hands. Bend your shoulders.
Open-minded	Face towards the other person. Stand close. A lot of eye contact. Firm or long handshake. May even embrace when meeting someone.

(continued on next page)

How you feel	What you look like to others
Sexual or romantic	Eye contact with a big smile. Laugh too much. Stare at your partner. Wink. Wet your lips. Move your legs. Thrust hips or chest. Consume more space. Touch yourself.
Surprised	Step back. Lean back with wide-opened eyes and mouth. Hold hands up with displayed palms. Touch your face.
Skeptical	Squint your eyes. Furrow your brow. Tilt your head slightly. Turn your head down. Tighten your lips.
Worry	Pace. Fidget. Rub your face. Run your hands through your hair. Cannot focus. Do repetitive actions.

As we work to improve our body language, we should start with self-compassion. This may allow us to relate to ourselves using a non-judgmental, patient, and kindhearted attitude that is specific to our perceived shortcomings. When we care, forgive, and are kind to ourselves, we can reduce critical and punishing thoughts about ourselves. Our nonverbal communication will tell others a lot about our most inner feelings, beliefs, and thoughts. Self-compassion can even "buffer" negative feedback specific to body comparison and body appreciation.

As we seek to express ourselves, many opt for cosmetic surgery for physical modifications. For others, less costly—maybe—and less invasive procedures are preferred. At a minimum, some of us are only willing to cut or color our hair to express ourselves and tell others something about us. This woman's hairstyle and color in the photo are modest, yet she adds a flower. Her pearls and lacy blouse complete her portrait.

Getty Images

Wait! Did you see a lacy blouse? Look again. Tattoos allow people to nonverbally communicate "in a radical way . . . using their bodies as a means of communication," according to Kertzman et al. (2019). Body markers, including tattoos, convey information—about the people who have them and how others view and judge them. We have been tattooing our bodies for a long time. You might be surprised that this photo dates back more than one hundred years—1907, actually. More recent work (Kertzman et al., 2019) on "women with tattoos" finds that those with tattoos have significantly lower self-esteem between the "ideal body, ideal self, and tattooed woman" status. While younger generations have become more accepting of tattoos, others view them as foolish and a waste of money. Tattooing one's body is a visual representation of interpersonal communication and is also linked to self-esteem associated with physical appearance. Findings also suggest that there is a large perception and judgment gap between women with and women without tattoos.

Interestingly, one study finds that older women associate their tattoos with their self-esteem—even if their tattoos conjured negative or emotional reactions. Several (48 percent) share that their subsequent tattoo removal was done in part to improve their self-esteem. Researchers also find an increase in self-esteem after tattoo removal specific to acceptance of one's body. Others with tattoos, however, state that these markers make them feel unique and emphasize individuality.

Tattoos, for many, are seen as an enhancement of one's body and its image. Many report a boost in self-esteem and uniqueness after their first tattoo. This "artificial decoration" has both self-image and nonverbal communication implications. These permanent markings are intentional, visible, and say something about the wearer. Tattoos are even referenced alongside breast implants, tummy tucks, and Botox as a way to enhance the body and create the "perfect" or ideal. As we know, cultural standards and biases are a part of how tattoos are used and perceived, and we start developing our biases and perceptions at a young age.

CRADLE TO COFFIN NONVERBAL COMMUNICATION

Do you realize that we engage in body processing as early as three months of age? Our brains and eyes seek to understand different types of body-relevant information and interpret what postural positions mean. Think about how physically close we position our faces with a baby's face. We display animated facial expressions and may even touch the baby to strengthen positive communication and bond. In return, babies wiggle, coo, and gaze back at us.

Nonverbal language development starts in infancy and a baby's social environment influences pre-linguistic vocalizations. This is true for many animals. As babies consume their environment through visual, auditory, and touch stimuli, their babbling exhibits pitch and rhythm changes based on social conditions and adult interactions. Over time, babies will mimic older individuals during face-to-face interactions and take turns communicating with their adult caregivers. These early nonverbal behaviors are important for development.

"Even very young infants are capable of making virtually all of the facial movements involved in these (specific) patterns" (Barrett, 1993). In infancy, facial expressions directly reflect the baby's emotion and state of being—meaning, when a baby feels upset, we can clearly see this displayed on their face and in their body language.

Infants are able to recognize differences in smiles as a part of understanding emotions from their caregivers (Sauter, 2017). Sadly, when babies miss out on physical interactions with others, this tactile deprivation negatively affects socio-cognitive development. Dr. Harry Harlow's well-known 1932 behavioral science study on infant rhesus monkeys and maternal attachment is a prime example of this. Dr. Harlow separated infant rhesus monkeys from their natural mothers and raised them with "mothers" made out of either cloth or wire. He discovered that without real mothers or live touch, the infant monkeys developed social deficits. Therefore, maternal separation, social isolation, and dependency were deemed important for social and cognitive development. His findings on the importance of touch in infant development laid the groundwork for hundreds of subsequent studies validating basic tactile needs. We are sensitive at an early age to various types of social contact signals. When we gaze, touch, and vocalize with infants, their bodily self-awareness increases.

"From four to five months of age, infants also prefer to listen to their own name rather than other names. They use this nonverbal as a social cue to guide their attention to events and objects in the external world" (Hazem et al., 2018). And what a world it is that consumes them. From infancy through childhood and adolescence, nonverbal displays help us navigate relationships, conquer challenges, and build our self-worth.

As children, we are besieged for hours a day with images from our television and on social media. Children between ages two and five spend thirty-two hours a week in front of the television. It's practically a full-time job (McDonough, 2009). Adolescents clock twenty-eight hours, on average, in front of the TV. Lengthy time in front of the television can have a negative impact on body image, and, thus, how we communicate through our nonverbals. Cartoon characters are drawn out of proportion. Magazine ads tell us how to dress. Commercials sing us into the "ideal" everything. Advertisers perpetuate the importance of thinness and beauty. Millions are spent on diet ads—thereby confirming the idea that we must lose weight. Our physical bodies are under constant attack and yet we seek validations and answers from the same sources that perpetuate this onslaught.

Early stage development marks a delicate time for negative body image. In studies, children who focus on body functionality value their bodies beyond appearance and objectification. Meaning, if we teach about the healthy functions of each body part instead of the perception of being perfect as a whole, then we are able to develop self-esteem and acceptance. An emphasis on body functionality reinforces in children the power of performance and ability rather than the importance of looks and social affirmation.

Body image is a part of how we define ourselves and is crucial for development. We want to feel valued and accepted by others. Adolescence also marks a time of intense physical changes to our bodies and experts confirm that as girls grow older, they become more dissatisfied with their bodies, and many girls profess that they wish to be thinner. However, boys are not as vulnerable to this puberty phenomena in that they see growth changes as muscular development rather than fat attainment.

"Perceptions of appearance emerge as the strongest single indicator of self-esteem among female adolescents" (Kertman et al., 2019). Research suggests a strong link between women and body appreciation at a much higher significance than for men. It's a shame that we fail to aggressively promote self-compassion through self-kindness, a belief in humanity, and mindfulness—all that may contribute to positive body image and less destructive behaviors.

"Self-objectification may increase opportunities for girls and women to experience higher body shame, more appearance anxiety, reduced concentration on mental and physical tasks, and decreased awareness of internal bodily states" (Calogero and Pina, 2011). That's a notable finding and quite alarming for both developing young girls and women navigating their worlds. Calogero and Pina conclude that compounded body shaming experiences can lead to high rates of depression, sexual dysfunctions, and eating disorders. Studies also confirm that women report greater levels of self-guilt and body guilt compared to men.

Body shaming, the degree to which "women feel ashamed of their bodies when they perceive them as falling short of feminine beauty ideals," emanates through our nonverbal communication and it's disturbing (Calogero and Pina, 2011). This is painful—to know that we "fall short" merely based on the evaluation of ourselves and the harsh judgments of our peers. How, many ask, do we begin to "fix" ourselves as we continue down life's path?

According to the research, women's dissatisfaction with their own bodies happens across a life span. On a positive note, the obsession with physical appearance and reaching the "ideal" appears to decrease with age.

Webster and Tiggemann (2003) find that, as women age, they think more about control over their bodies and come to understand that it is not as important as it was earlier. Thus, their overall views and feelings about themselves change. While the authors reference this change as perhaps "lowering their expectations," a degree of body acceptance and self-evaluation help with self-image. It is even suggested that, "cognitive control provides that protective mechanism." Improved levels of self-concept and self-esteem happen when we use our brains instead of others' judgments of us.

Alleva et al. (2014) find that mature women are significantly more satisfied with their body functionality than younger women. They suggest that, as we age, appearance becomes less important. Physical health and body function fitness take center stage.

MEDIA MAYHEM

Let's face it, the media constantly bombards us with unrealistic body ideals—only adding to the vicious cycle of body dissatisfaction. And much of this happens through the influence of visuals and nonverbal messages. Look at print ads. Watch the people in commercials. Women also tend to battle stereotyping, prejudgment, and bias more than men. The constant assault of ideal women on television, magazines, and social media lead to negative feelings about our bodies. In turn, we pay the physical and emotional price.

While we can be rather astute at "critically processing media images" without consciously doing so, we are lured into the nonverbal messages that saturate our senses. We like to think that we are disconnected from the negative influences around us. But, in reality, we are trapped in these webs.

Negative and long-lasting effects from exposure to idealized media images are well documented.

Facebook, Instagram, and other social media sites focus on nonverbal visual imagery. Actually, Instagram's platform caters to the posting of photos and videos meant to capture and retain viewers without the requirement of text to explain the images. Instagram has a detrimental impact on young adult women's body image (Tiggemann and Barbato, 2018). Social media even encourages observers to comment on others' photos, thereby perpetuating this unhealthy cycle focused in on outward appearances. Appearance-based comments on social media are the norm. The sheer number of "likes" on Facebook are often viewed as being specific to compliments on the subject's appearance only feed into a vicious cycle of posting and liking.

One study finds that compliments about appearance improve women's moods, but then increases body shaming feelings and fuels the quest to post something prettier and "better" next time. These photo-based social platforms are intimately linked to body surveillance and self-objectification. Social media platforms provide ways to compare ourselves with others and how the posted comments make us feel is usually negative.

Credit: Patrik Nygren, www.flickr.com

Women tend to invest a significant amount of time taking selfies from "the right angle" and then editing them with filters and face-altering apps in order to obtain the "most desired" photo to post for others to view and comment on. And the chosen filter usually ensures that we have huge eyes, flawless skin, and delicate noses. After posting photos, females spend considerable time reading what others write and scrutinizing the number of times their videos are viewed, or photos are given a "heart" or "like" rating.

When observers write text on appearance-based photos, people usually comment by saying "looking good" or some other beauty-based, physical assessment—even "heart" and "thumbs up" emoticons tell the nonverbal opinion. Comments on photos of people are seldom character-based like "you look happy" or "life is treating you well." Rather, we read comments based on physical appearance, such as "you look hot," or "I like your hair." These are not healthy forms of communication.

Remember that emoticons are used to reflect their user's personality and social behaviors. Duan et al. (2018) point out that emoticons "speed up the communication because they allow users to convey more information about emotions in less time." These cryptic symbols help us understand the meaning of text beyond words while assessing behavior as well. This is an influential part of communication. We would be wise to understand these deeper nonverbal messaging opportunities.

Social media provides a platform in which appearance can be the center of attention. On average, women age sixteen to twenty-five years spend up to five hours each week taking selfies and sharing them on social media sites (Mills et al., 2018). Beyond time consumption, the sheer amount of time devoted to editing and retouching selfies has a potentially huge negative impact on a female's self-esteem, body image, and how she communicates.

Mills and others (2018) find that mood and self-image are negatively impacted as a result of taking and posting selfies on the Internet. A vicious cycle of taking the "perfect" photo and posting untouched images leads to more anxiety, less confidence, and thoughts of feeling less attractive after posting. Then, the anxiety of waiting for "likes" and comments perpetuates the cycle. What if the selfie isn't "liked" a lot? Should I just crop my face or leave my body in for comments? Do I look fat? How different do I look from the re-touched photo?

Additionally, posting re-touched selfies does not increase confidence. This only continues the cycle of appearance-based judgments and bad feelings. Let's look at one study that examined factors specific to selfies and our bodies—anxiety, depression, confidence, feelings of fatness, physical attractiveness, and satisfaction with body size. The findings are clear—selfie posts increase women's anxiety levels while decreasing their confidence and lowering their perceptions of their physical attractiveness. (Mills et al., 2018).

Facebook is the most popular form of social media in the world. Modica (2019) finds that, "women make more extreme upward comparisons through social media compared to in-person" comparisons. Furthermore, the frequency of posting on Facebook is associated with increases in body dissatisfaction. The literature literally calls frequent selfie taking and posting a "risky on-line health-related behavior"—especially in terms of mental health.

"Anything that focuses attention on external appearance . . . can produce negative consequences" (Tiggemann and Barbato, 2018). Selfies (self-posing) are directly linked to women and girls' views of self and body concerns per the literature. Women judge themselves against media standards and almost always are left disappointed, knowing they cannot attain beauty and size standards required of the ideal.

Women in the media can be up to twenty percent below the expected body weight and still be considered the "ideal thin" (Watson et al., 2019). For example, *Vogue* magazine almost always features excessively thin women in images that capture our attention. And it works. We associate the thinness and attractiveness of the models with wealth, status, and luxury—and measure these body language factors against our own look and status. Not surprisingly, women's magazines have ten times more articles and ads about weight loss than men's magazines.

"The pressure to be slim is continually reinforced both by advertising and by peers . . . We are continually bombarded by images of thin, happy people" (Stephens, Hill, and Hanson, 1994). As researchers point out, "the current ideal womanly shape is bean lean, slender as the night, narrow as an arrow, and pencil thin." Really? Talk about a setup—how slender is the night, honestly.

Print media is notorious for promoting negative body images—perhaps more so than television. Not only do "perfect" women grace the covers on magazines displaying satisfied body language, but these very same magazines then offer "beauty tips, tools, and techniques" so we can better ourselves—or at least look better. Calogero and Pina (2011) offer some sage advice in that we must find ways to "value women's bodies for more than their potential sexual attraction and appearance." We must ensure that the messages our nonverbals convey promote positive body images and authentic happiness and contentment regardless of the written message.

Courtesy of Kirschner Amao

"You look beautiful."
I startle at the compliment. Then I smile. "I'm beautiful to the one person who matters."
She nods. "Hector's mouth is going to drop open when he sees you."
"I hope so. But I meant me. I'm beautiful to me."

—Rae Carson, *The Bitter Kingdom*

CHAPTER 2

How to Read Other Women's Body Language

When you see another woman, you know immediately what she is thinking. Without hesitation, she evokes an emotional response from your core.

"People rapidly and spontaneously make judgments about the personality of others based on appearance cues" (Hess, 2016). Whether we like it or not, physical appearance and body language matter.

As we discussed in Chapter 1, reading body language has a lot to do with our appearance and visual stimuli. We form first impressions very quickly—especially judging facial cues and facial expression cues. When we are able to see someone's face, we make fewer errors in deciphering their body language cues. Obstructed faces present a challenge for us. Proverbio et al. (2018) finds that men are slower perceptual processors of gestures when they cannot see facial expressions compared to women. Actually, there are several gender-based differences in body language and nonverbal communication, in both sending and receiving information. Regardless, women constantly compare themselves to other people—especially to other women.

We self-evaluate by comparing ourselves to others, which is known as social comparison theory. Specific to body image, we assess ourselves through perceptions of upward or downward comparisons (Gillen and Lefkowitz, 2011). Meaning, we liken ourselves with others to determine who is "better off." Who has the better body? Which one of us is nicer? Who has more friends? Why do they gravitate to her more? The thoughts that roll through our heads cause us to constantly question how we fit in and how other people perceive us. Oddly enough, this is normal for pack animals and we, after all, are social creatures.

Credit: Pedro Ribeiro Simões, www.flickr.com

Two subtypes of social comparison theory consider how we judge our bodies against others. We use both upward and downward comparisons. Specifically, upward social comparisons are when we compare ourselves to others and believe we are superior. When we use downward social comparisons, we believe we are inferior to others. Even though we know it is detrimental and emotionally unhealthy to compare ourselves to someone else, we still do it. And it's usually based only on appearance comparisons.

To better understand nonverbal communication and making social inferences, we should consider the "perception of action, intention, emotion, and other aspects of social cognition" (Balas et al., 2012). In simple terms, we need to pay attention to many factors about other people simultaneously—including how they feel, what they think, and their intentions. Researchers find that we are able to detect authentic engagement through someone's behaviors and nonverbal clues. Actually, almost two-thirds of any social encounter comes from nonverbal cues (Brook and Servatka, 2016).

In social situations, we adjust our own behaviors based on the nonverbals we are observing from others. We can pick up on non-verbals with only a "thin-slice" of behavior. High levels of social inference are made via our body language—including facial gestures and nonverbal cues.

Through various movements, we use nonverbals to express ourselves. These may include touch, posture, facial expressions, and other body parts, but we must also consider hair style, clothing choices, and adornments as part of our communication choices.

Getty Images

Let's examine the body language in this picture. What do you see? How do you feel about these three females? Are their smiles genuine? Are they making eye contact with the camera? Do you like their hairstyles? What do you think about the degree of them touching each other? Would you consider them close friends? What emotions would you assign to each woman? Do you subconsciously rate their attractiveness? Are you trying to figure out their ethnicities? How do you judge this photo? So many pieces of nonverbal information to consider in a single image—and we do it quickly. We actually do this—and a lot more—every time we engage with another woman.

"We are not wired to assimilate information and simply suspend judgments until a careful, reasoned assessment occurs" (Patterson, 2017). We actually make quick, snap judgments, which tend to lead us to like people who are similar to us. As a part of this quick reaction to others, we compare ourselves to the "ideal" self—for ourselves and with others. Known as self-discrepancy theory, we have a set of internalized "standards" of what is perfect (ideal) and compare ourselves to these standards. If there's a big gap between our two perceptions of ideal and real, we experience emotional turmoil. For some women, this chronically distressful state consumes them—making them feel consistently inadequate.

To add to this, social media platforms constantly provide opportunities for social comparisons—including subjecting users to unrealistic beauty and body expectations and judgments from other women. Too often, shame is the emotion elicited as a result of negative social media posting. How often have you looked at an Instagram photo of a female and studied it a bit longer to look for flaws? Or what do you think when you see two female friends on Facebook laughing with each other and wonder why you're not included? When you see your favorite couple dressed up and out to dinner captured in a photograph, do you look longer at her appearance or his? Mostly likely the other woman is the focus of your attention. You study all the details of her dress, makeup, hair, body posture, and facial expressions to determine if you like what you see.

We are aware that these snap judgments are both quick and long lasting. When we think about the impressions we form, we often think about first impressions. These strong nonverbal and visual cues leave emotional and cognitive imprints on our brain. In just one-tenth of a second, we are able to look at a face, read its expressions, and draw conclusions—real or perceived, good or bad. Our social preferences are almost instantaneous. Sadly, negative impressions often carry more weight than their positive counterparts.

It doesn't take much for us to judge. Willis and Todorov's (2006) well-known research on rapid facial exposure impressions says that it doesn't take a lot of time for us to infer traits about someone with minimal exposure time. Specifically, five easily understood traits tell us a lot about someone. Let's do a little experiment based on two similar photographs (see below) of white, blonde, long-haired women with no other information about them. Quickly look at each face as you consider the following trait-based questions and answer with a quick "yes" or "no."

Trait	What You're Thinking As You Look At Her
Trustworthiness	*Do I trust her? Yes or No?*
Competence	*Do I think she has knowledge and skills? Yes or No?*
Likeability	*Do I like her? Yes or No?*
Attractiveness	*Is she pretty? Yes or No?*
Aggressiveness	*Is she aggressive? Yes or No?*

Answering "yes" or "no" quickly about each question is easy. But, if you look longer at each photo, your answers might change. Believe it or not, we are able to make up our minds in one-tenth of a second about these five traits. Within a couple of seconds, we form a strong impression about the other person. And, with a little more time, perhaps two to three seconds, we actually rationalize as

Getty Images

Getty Images

to why we made these judgements. Perhaps you justify your answers with thoughts like these:

> I liked her smile and her straight teeth, so I thought she was attractive.

> Her bright, big hairstyle drew me in, so I considered her prettier than the other woman.

> I didn't like the tilt of her head, so I questioned her believability or competence.

> Her smile was genuine and she has expressive eyes, so I found her to be trustworthy.

Some findings even posit that when we want to gain acceptance into a group, our smiles significantly increase the chances of "hanging out with" the group. Physical distance (proxemics) is also associated with social acceptance. The very fact that these two images are next to each other would have made you compare the two women without me having to ask you to consciously think about it. Women judge value based on ranking themselves against other women.

Of course, these judgements have little to do with being an intelligent observer, but they are strongly associated with social intelligence and nonverbal communication. In saying this, Montiel et al. (2017) suggest that:

People who develop strong first impressions are less prone to depressive symptoms, less social anxiety, and shyness. They also tend to be "more socially competent, open to experiences, more confident, more expressive, and communicative."

So, good news on the horizon for women's body language and feelings of worth—perhaps. Now, what do we do with our bodies to accurately communicate what's in our minds?

HAND IT TO HER

"Females are emotionally more expressive than males" (Steephen, Mehta, and Bapi, 2018). No shock there! We connect expressiveness and emotions and then judge others based on what we see and feel. The stereotypical mindset that women are more emotional may also make others more sensitive to women's behaviors based on this presumption—or fact.

Women are frequently known for "talking with their hands." These nonverbal displays of gesticulating are important for two reasons. Gesturing with our hands and arms allows us to communicate what we are thinking without using our words. Additionally, gesturing affirms or voids a verbal message—when the two are in conflict, we default to the nonverbal and dismiss the verbal message.

We typically use specific body gestures to communicate our message. Sauter (2017) provides observable nonverbals associated with the two positive emotions of elation and pride.

Positive emotions	What we notice
Elation **(based on an unexpected positive event)**	Smiles with widened eye aperture, raised eyebrows and smiles, high-intensity dynamic expressions, high body, fast and expansive body movements, arms stretched out, head tilted back and up.
Pride **(based on completion of a goal)**	Expanded posture, head tilt back, small smile, combination of postural and body cues.

These nonverbal movements of the hands and/or arms are an external support for verbal or vocal communication. For example, if we notice a woman saying, "ummm," she might also be holding her arms up with her palms open as if to say, "I don't know. Maybe?" A shoulder shrug may reinforce this message of uncertainty.

When we gesture with our hands, arms, and head, we signal a host of emotions towards the person or people with whom we are communicating. These movements can be connected to both nonverbal and verbal cues depending on their function. Three specific gesture functions include emblems, illustrators, and regulators.

Emblems back up what we say. For example, we verbalize "okay," and our hand gesture makes the "okay" sign by touching the thumb and index finger together with other fingers stretched apart.

Illustrators give a quick "illustration" and provide direction. For example, motioning your hand towards the restroom provides direction without you saying anything.

Regulators are gestures that help the person speaking regulate or keep time. For example, you share a story and as you talk about the "first thing," you raise your hand holding up one finger to demonstrate "one" and continue raising fingers as you count higher.

Can you guess what each of these hand gestures communicate?

Iconic gestures illustrate something physical and add details to what is said. When this type of gesturing synchronizes with the verbal message it is often associated with honesty. If not synchronized, we may unconsciously question the message and wonder

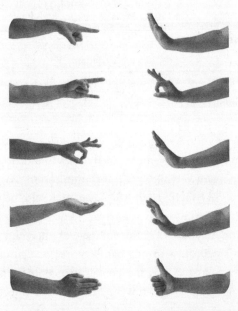

Getty Images

if the person is being manipulative or deceptive. For example, if someone is cold, we expect him or her to wrap their arms around their body or even rub their hands to generate heat.

We also use gestures in specific situations. Before we learn to speak, we point to objects to let others know that we want something. Needless to say, we continue with these types of nonverbal (deictic) gestures into adulthood.

A special set of metaphoric gestures provide visual representation for abstract ideas—like clenching your fists to let others know that you are frustrated or upset. Or shaking your finger to illustrate your frustration. We'll even tap our foot if we're nervous or anxious. Rhythm-based gestures are indicative of beat gestures.

Gesturing allows us to visually describe a situation or object in addition to emphasizing or silently confirming a verbal message. When gestures and speech are combined, we "process simultaneously to form a single representation" (Dargue and Sweller, 2018). We also do this without much cognitive effort.

CAN YOU READ MY BODY?

No single indicator of body language should be interpreted without considering other nonverbals. Just because someone scratches their nose or shifts their eyes doesn't mean we "know" what's really going on with their behavior, mood, or intentions. It's important to establish baselines of behavior for how people behave and act. Once we see how people "normally or typically" behave, we can then gain a better understanding of them and when they deviate from their baselines. Body language is a complex science which requires a certain frame of mind, reference, and ability in order to interpret through the use of our senses and cognitive abilities. We should look for clusters of nonverbal clues to determine what someone is thinking or feeling. Some call this the "rule of four" (Wilson, 2009). Although we look for three or four cues, keep in mind that reading body language does not happen in isolation. One nonverbal may trigger you to react in a specific manner, but remember to look for additional cues (the rule of four).

"Nonverbal behaviors often cannot be mapped onto specific meanings with any certainty" because we need to also consider motive or intent, control, status, and expectations (Hall, Coats, and Smith-LeBeau, 2005). As experts point out, nonverbal behaviors are often "tacit and unconscious." We just understand them without really thinking or talking about it. Some call this a "sixth sense" or "gut feeling."

Women are extremely sensitive to nonverbals and are often skilled at decoding them. For example, friendly behavior tends to be classified as "female" whereas emotional stability is associated as "male" according to Koppensteiner and Grammer (2011). Gender stereotypes are alive and often promoted in today's society. No doubt we can be both friendly and emotionally stable; however, it may not be that simple. When we try to make sense of body language, we operate from three coordinated networks (Kana and Travers, 2012). Specifically:

1. Visuomotor aspects of the body language: our brains coordinate body movements through visual perceptions.
2. Reflex-like emotional responses: these are nearly instantaneous reactions based on how we feel.
3. Proprioceptive responses: our emotional and physical responses using our body language.

With almost cat-like reactions, we are able to simultaneously look at another woman, gauge her movements, feel something, and physically react. It's quick and often involuntary. This rapid and automatic emotional processing of body postures is innate and primal. Our inner brains—our limbic region (our emotional centers)—are all activated. The amygdala within our limbic regions are hyper-sensitive—especially to fear and negative emotions. Experts find that non-fear based emotions may actually activate different regions of our brains other than the amygdala.

"Happy body language is found to elicit increased activation of the visual cortex and not the amygdala" (Kana and Travers, 2012). Seeing someone happy may stimulate our visual brains rather than our trigger-happy emotional limbic brains. Just by looking at a woman smiling, our emotions are triggered. Additionally, isn't it funny that when we smile with slightly opened mouths, we look just a tad bit happier? Do you see slightly opened mouths displayed by four women in the photo below? You can't miss them. They appear even happier than the others.

Getty Images

By watching facial expressions and how the body moves, we glean important information from every interaction. Our nonverbal cues express gender-specific language and provide important clues for each gender. Studies find that women smile more and make more eye contact. Men tend to smile less and make less eye contact. Men tend to initiate touch and take up more space compared to women.

When we use nonverbals, our message is enhanced. Our unique, and not so unique, communication skills and styles of expression carry psychological significance during social interactions. "How we say things with our body postures and movements, facial expressions, gestures, touching, eye contact, use of space, and so on" help us build rapport with others (Spangler, 1995). Nonverbal communication has a greater impact than spoken words. Spangler writes, "Although we use both verbal and non-verbal communication, we may consciously attend to the verbal but gain more feedback from the nonverbal." He also explains, "When there are gaps between verbal and nonverbal behavior, it is commonly held that the information from the nonverbal behavior is more valid, more truthful, and more revealing." More valid? More truthful? More revealing? Wow!

IN SYNC: THE RELATIONSHIP, NOT THE BAND

Homophily is the love of the same—age, gender, socioeconomic status, personal beliefs, or other defining characteristics. As a basic principle of biology, we want to be around people who are like us. From friendships to romantic interests, we are unconsciously and visually drawn to aspects of other women without really understanding why.

"There's something about the company of women that gets us through it" (Lancaster, 2001). When we interact with other women, we don't talk about solving each other's problems, per se, it's more about comfort, time, support, solace, empathy, and emotional relief. Most women interact with other women out of necessity—it fills an emotional gap at a core level when we engage with our same sex. Research confirms that, when faced with stress or challenging situations, we seek social contact—we "tend and befriend"—and female relationships are just the ticket.

"Rapport occurs when a relationship is in harmony," according to Matsumoto, Frank, and Hwang (2013). By being "on the same page" as fellow women, we are able to ascertain information, make social connections, and reinforce relationships. Experts suggest that we build rapport through mirroring other women, invoking a sense of obligation (favors), and finding commonalities. As a result, a few of these women become valued members of our in-group and we "build a sense of camaraderie." Thus, "mutual trust and friendship" develops among women who spend a lot of time together.

When we naturally and authentically display rapport-building nonverbal actions, we draw in others, especially women who may want to connect with us. Matsumoto, Frank, and Hwang (2013) suggest we use the following nonverbals to build rapport with other women.

The Nonverbal	Why We Should Display These to Her
Smiling	Duchenne (authentic smile with crinkles corners of the eyes and smiling with the mouth) smiles go a long way as women watch other women and read their body language. We expect our smile to be returned.
Direct body orientation	Face her to demonstrate genuine intentions and interest. Women prefer to be approached head on, not from the side, and especially not from men.
Uncrossed arms and legs	Women watch how other women cross and uncross. This unconscious crossing behavior is associated with open or closed mindsets in that her body does what her mind thinks. This nonverbal also can diffuse defensiveness.
Symmetrical arms	Anytime we produce symmetrical actions, we give the perception of being "in balance" and in control of our emotions. Women should also master not tilting their heads when engaged with another person. Bending the head or other body parts breaks symmetry and we don't like it.
Moderate eye contact	Eye contact with women elicits feelings of connectedness and interest. This shows her that you are interested without staring or being aloof by looking away.
Forward leaning posture	When someone or something interests us, we move our bodies forward to show engagement. Leaning in lets a woman know we want to be a part of what she is doing or saying.
Touch	Women have more freedom to touch other women. A hug, a handshake, or similar gesture physically connects women. Touch lets her know that we want to build trust. Of course, we must always be aware of touch intentions, body location, length of touch, and who initiates.

We need to build strong rapport with trusted women because it helps us to "create a platform for credible information" and engages us—both personally and professionally.

To strengthen our interpersonal relationships, we might also want to "focus on and remember our smiling, gazing, and nodding because these behaviors are pleasant and desirable" (Hall et al., 2007). I know, conversations are complex, so thinking that a simple smile will do the trick is questionable. However, smiles are universally understood and carry merit—especially when they are authentic. The payoff is worth the investment.

PALPABLE PEER POWER

We are drawn to those who comfort us and lay the groundwork for building relationships. As a part of this, women are almost always better at decoding our nonverbal cues and understanding ourselves than men.

"Women are usually more comfortable with higher levels of nonverbal involvement in interactions, especially in same-sex interactions" (Patterson, 2017). We use our open body postures to show others that we are in control of ourselves—even when we want to nonverbally express power and dominance.

While some experts posit that female role models may make other women feel inferior given their own levels of professional success, the majority of the literature suggests that women benefit from exposure and support of successful female leaders. When these women present themselves as powerful and influential within their spheres, others take notice and are often inspired. One study that looked at women under stressful conditions found that they exhibited "empowered behaviors when exposed to female leader role models" (Latu et al., 2019).

When strong and successful female role models are visible to other women, it produces empowering effects. Female observers often mimic the nonverbals of powerful women. Can you identify the leader in this photo? What body language and other nonverbal clues do you see?

Getty Images

Look at the use of space, posture, as well as arm, hand, and leg positions. The woman on the right of this photo takes up a lot of space, as she casually drapes her arm across the empty chair. Her posture is relaxed, and her feet do not angle towards the other women. Her right hand is slightly open with a bent wrist. Her left hand rests comfortably on her lap. She is secure in this meeting. The other women position their bodies directly towards her with all their hands on the table. Their smiles confirm that they are "ready," and let her know they are authentically engaged with her. Both even lean in to confirm their interest. Clearly, the woman on the right is leading this meeting.

Let's decode another photo on the next page. While we can't see their entire bodies, their use of hands, placement of their arms, and seating positions provide enough clues. You probably believe that the woman in the middle is leading this brainstorming session. The other two women touch their chins to demonstrate interest while they evaluate what she says. They are actually mirroring each other too. The outer two women also display slightly tilted down heads as if to let the middle woman know that she's in charge. Even though the center female is physically smaller, the wide placement of her left arm tells us that she is okay with consuming space.

Getty Images

When other women do well, we would be well-served to watch and learn from them. Visible and powerful women leaders can function as positive role models to help other women grow in leadership capacities, and it doesn't take a lot of effort to assist other women. For the most part, it's a visual solution. Basically, "female leader role models can show women how to behave in challenging situations—how to speak, stand, or move" (Latu et al., 2018). In return, other women's feelings of belonging and self-confidence develop. This process is called "empowering mimicry" in that imitating other women's nonverbal behaviors will empower us—particularly during challenging situations. If you can see it, you can be it.

It is worth noting, though, that these behaviors and feelings are not always the same for men. Men are not empowered by the visibility of strong male role models. It appears that their feelings of empowerment and leadership are rather constant—regardless of role model visibility. "Women are the ones affected by stereotype threat" within leadership roles (Latu et al., 2019). Stereotype threat is when someone "is in a situation or doing something for which a negative stereotype about one's group applies" (Steele, 1997).

And, because of this, the threat of others' judgments will negatively impact the person who is often stereotyped.

When we like someone, our human (animal) nature is to mimic or mirror her or him. From facial expressions to body postures, we seek congruence by matching others' behaviors. It's a subtle, yet impactful, way that we connect and flatter each other. Basically, it's mentally saying, "I like you, so I act like you." This chameleon effect increases positive feelings and builds "harmonious social interactions" as well as "appropriate responses to situations" (Latu et al., 2019). Mimicry is often an unconscious behavior. We don't really think about it—it just happens—unless we are intentionally stopping it.

Society has a prescribed set of norms and rules which help us to understand our place in the world as well as to comprehend how we interact with others. We are able to quickly interpret the unspoken meaning of sadness, fear, disgust, surprise, contempt, and anger. These are, for the most part, universally recognized nonverbals emitted by facial expressions and body movements. Whether it's the 1960s or 2020s, some facial expressions are timeless and require no words for comprehension. What is the young woman below saying in each photo? You know these emotions.

It's what we chose to focus on that usually changes the meaning of an interaction. Situations with our peers provide the potential for things to go well or to take a nosedive into conflict and emotional distress. Regardless, we want to be heard and understood. Peers also play a large role in our beliefs about body image and self-esteem. Female college students report "fearing" negative judgments by their peers; in turn, these women have lower self-esteem and body image issues.

Courtesy of Billie

Women judge each other on attractiveness. Additionally, women frequently adjust and edit their bodies during social interactions to create the desired nonverbal impressions on their audience (Mills et al., 2018). We often do this through primping in a mirror or posting images and videos on social media. The picture-perfect selfie or photograph is edited through the angle of the camera (higher for thinner chins and longer necks), and the selection of background, facial expression, and body position. This self-presentation behavior is a part of our impression management. We want to have control of our image and shape others' views of us. Heck, we even wiggle into "shapewear" in an attempt to control and persuade our bodies into the "right" figure. In turn, women "police" and self-scrutinize their bodies—knowing that our peers are judging us based on appearance. And our body language reinforces these mindsets.

By being intentional with our nonverbal actions, both senders and receivers reap the benefits. Women, in particular, who hold "open, expansive body postures subsequently show increases in self-reported feelings of power," according to Latu (2019) and colleagues. These same women also make more "risky, reward-oriented decisions." For example, if you use confident body language, like erect posture and direct eye contact, then you might be willing to ask for that raise. Or if you hold your head high and own the fact you are the most knowledgeable one in the group then you might be singled out for additional praise or benefits. When women display expansive body postures, their feelings of empowerment increase. This is important to know for reducing fear and feelings of negativity that too many of us feel when stressed or "under the microscope." And, let's face it, we are often under the lens of scrutiny in many situations.

COLOR AND CULTURE CAVEATS

Societal norms are formidable, and they often dictate the definition of beauty and who we "should" find attractive. If we fail to agree or adhere to these standards, then we are likely to struggle with body satisfaction issues. Mucherah and Frazier (2013) find that "societal norms partly equate women's stature to their appearance and, consequently, attractiveness." Women also associate their employment status with self-esteem and body dissatisfaction. Too often we are stereotyped based on external aspects—including our gender and our race.

While society has made advances in embracing various ethnicities and providing "equal opportunities," race remains a sensitive topic. Defined in this book, race refers to a person's "physical characteristics, such as bone structure and skin, hair, or eye color. An example of race is brown, white, or black skin (all from various parts of the world)" (diffen.com).

Courtesy of Gemma Chua-Tran

Let's talk about a topic in our society that specifically has to do with women and their relationship to race. While we share the label of "women," the unique shades of our skin separate many of us when it comes to perceptions, judgements, and the like. In particular, the research I share paints an ugly picture of how some women are viewed simply based on their race.

We are at a disadvantage due to multiple sources of oppression like race, gender, religion, and other traits according to intersectionality theory. This nonverbally appears through gender-based racial microaggressions. When race, gender, and other traits overlap, there is systemic oppression and discrimination. It's like a double-whammy.

Adding to this, objectification theory indicates that women are often reduced to their body appearance and sexual attributes. In numerous studies, researchers find that skin color determines self-worth and black women suffer from social disadvantages. Even financially poor women with lighter skin have higher levels of self-esteem than wealthier darker-skinned women. The preference for lighter skin is evident from both black and white respondents.

Lighter skin tones are linked to higher job and education outcomes. Race is clearly associated with beauty and perceptions of superiority (Winter et al., 2019).

Watson et al., (2019) looked at unique black women indicators like hair, skin tone, and body type to gather information about body image and perceptions. They found that black women tend to spend a large amount of money and time on their hair and believe that "long, straight hair" is the desired look. Specific to skin tone, many believe that darker-skinned black women are "less attractive, less likely to achieve, and not suitable romantic partners" compared to lighter-skinned black women. In terms of body shape, the curvier body is perceived as "hypersexual" and objectified more versus the thin ideal.

Courtesy of Thought Catalog

For many women of color, it is difficult to navigate America's "white standards" of beauty while still respecting their unique cultural beliefs. Experts find that women who do not like the color of their skin do not like their overall bodies as well. Since a woman's merit is unfortunately linked to her appearance, it makes sense that our skin tone would also be a factor in this social norm.

"A tacit understanding is that darker skin, no matter one's starting point, is not advantageous," according to Mucherah and Frazier's (2013) work on the relationship between skin color, body image, and self-esteem among black women. All of these factors, while emotional or out of our control, play a role in body language and how women speak with their bodies. Does her skin glow? Is she radiant? Does she look happy? All of these questions are often not verbally answered because she emits the answers through her body language, facial expressions, and posture.

Fortunately, black history has had a "powerful and persistent influence on societal attitudes toward African American people" (Mucherah and Frazier, 2013). The literature suggests that black women may be less influenced by their peers than white women. Gillen and Lefkowitz (2011) suggest that black girls experience less peer jealously and competition in childhood. White women tend to idealize a thin body type, whereas Overstreet et al. (2010) find that black women are "more flexible" regarding their body shapes, weight, and definitions of beauty than non-black women.

Black women have lower rates of eating disorders and make fewer comparisons between intelligence, attractiveness, relationship success, and happiness than women of other races. They also do a better job at estimating men's preferred body type compared to white women's "ideal thin" beliefs. In addition, black women who watch black-oriented television shows have greater esteem for their own bodies.

Defining a curvaceous ideal includes consideration of breast size, buttock size, and weight, all of which many black women prefer to be larger than their white counterparts. White women state a preference for slender with medium size breasts. And, sadly, the further from this ideal, the greater their body dissatisfaction. By emphasizing the "ideal thin," all women lose the opportunity to embrace and celebrate others' standards of attractiveness.

White women often struggle with body satisfaction, the need to conceal their body size, weight-related depression, and anxiety. Black women, per the literature, have less preoccupation with weight and greater overall satisfaction with their bodies compared to other ethnicities. Yet, black women self-assess more negatively when exposed to attractive black models. One reason for this may be that music videos tend to feature sexualized, shapely, and slender body sizes.

Fortuitously, not all women want to be thin. Findings suggest that black women may consider how weight is distributed on the body as more important than overall size. The hourglass shape is considered more attractive and vital than being thin.

Courtesy of Eye for Ebony

Many white women believe that a thin waist is an "important marker of physical attractiveness" (Overstreet et al., 2010). Women with larger waists or smaller breasts tend to say that they are dissatisfied with this part of their bodies. Studies of *Playboy* magazine photos confirm that centerfold models usually have small waists with larger breasts and are considered "ideal" for what men want.

The vast majority of European women and Latin Americans state that they desire a thinner figure; no European women in the study said that she wished to be larger (Gillen and Lefkowitz,

2011). White women tend to fear getting fat, have a desire for thinness, and are preoccupied with their weight overall when compared to black women. Body mass index (BMI) yields interesting results in that black women have the most favorable overall body appreciation, including a preference for larger body size. This is the exact opposite of Asian women's emphasis on being thin.

Winter et al. (2019) posit that black female college students struggle more with body image if they attend predominantly white colleges. Asian women report similar body issues to white women, in addition to racially distinctive features like eyelid shape and size, as well as nose shape. Asian women also report a fear of gaining weight at higher rates than white women.

Credit: Noel Teo (CC BY 2.0)

Asian women may also internalize body dissatisfaction issues as a way of maintaining control and presenting a perceived desirable image of what they believe men would find attractive. In turn, they may appear more favorable for marriage. In many Asian cultures, "collectivism" is an important value; thus many Asian women may seek to assimilate to Western cultures in order to fit in. Straying from the norm is not acceptable. Per Winter and others' (2019) work, the "most requested plastic surgery procedures among Asian American women include rhinoplasties (nose reshaping) and eyelid surgeries." And, not surprisingly, requested modifications parallel stereotypical white features—including bigger eyes.

Results from hundreds of women of different races (white, black, Asian, Hispanic/Latina, and multiracial) self-reported their "favorite" and "least favorite" body parts. Even though all women struggle with body concerns, each female ethnicity group has unique feedback about themselves. While "favorite" body parts vary by race, the "least favorite" body part is the same—stomach/abs—for all five groups! And all, except black women, state that body size is their second least favorite part.

Race	"Favorite" body part	"Least favorite" body part
White women	Eye color	Stomach/abs
Black women	Lip thickness	Stomach/abs
Asian women	Hair overall	Stomach/abs
Hispanic/Latina women	Hair overall	Stomach/abs
Multiracial women	Lip thickness	Stomach/abs

Multiracial women report higher levels of body dissatisfaction than black and white women, including weight preoccupation and anxiety. Multiracial women, by the nature of their blended races and expectations, may struggle with the extreme concepts of being both "waifish" or "thick," and "too tanned" or "porcelain-skinned." Two distinct concepts of beauty based on body size and skin color present challenges for multiracial women. Hispanic/Latina women, compared to white women, did not have any significant differences in body image or body dissatisfaction.

When we are empowered and our self-esteem is secure, we think (cognitively) better, and our behaviors and actions appear to be within our control. We just feel better. Confidence and non-verbal displays of this help with our overall moods—which have cascading effects on others who we allow in our lives. Stand tall and be seen. Keep your body open and exude confidence. These action-mindset behaviors not only help us physically but impact our emotional well-being too.

Changing body image, thinness and weight ideals, and perceptions will not be easy. And we must remember that our attitude and belief biases are reliably detected through our body language. We know that stereotypes and prejudices are persistent through generations, and "stereotypes are resistant to being challenged" (Meadors and Murray, 2014).

These unconscious and subtle cues might be seen as microaggressions and are influenced when we interact with others. Starting with our emotions, personality, motivations, thoughts, and attitudes, our nonverbals and bodies communicate a lot of information. For the most part, this visible information reflects how we truly feel—more so than what we might actually say.

EMOTION POTION

Women tend to be better at decoding nonverbal information than men. However, Gulabovska and Leeson (2014) find that our emotional intelligence (EI) is a factor for understanding body language. When we understand others' nonverbal language, communication is more effective for both senders and receivers. The person who sends a nonverbal message is called the encoder and the decoder is the one who receives and interprets the message. Thereby, nonverbal communication is an interpersonal interaction.

"Nonverbal communication is a highly significant part of any interpersonal interaction" (Gulabovska and Leeson, 2014). A review of seventy-five studies conclude that women have an "advantage significantly exceeding chance." Therefore, we should use our interpersonal skills wisely in social encounters. We should also remember that women are able to read other women, and all are keenly aware of this. Most likely you've experienced this before in the company of women. For example, I bet this photo evokes emotions from you about her . . . and I'm thinking that they aren't positive.

Getty Images

Nonverbal decoding is an important social skill because it helps us to understand others' actions, emotions, and intentions. What do you think are the intentions of the female in this photo? Remember, she looks like she's in a workplace setting. Without a doubt—not professional!

Our proficiency at decoding nonverbal cues also gives us an advantage. Even the popular social science field of emotional intelligence requires superior decoding abilities from both sexes. Therefore, learning how to encode and decode cues gives us insights to unspoken thoughts and feelings. Not surprisingly, women also have greater levels of empathy and are deemed more adept than men at reading and understanding others' emotional expressions. As a part of emotional intelligence, women with higher scores display enhanced abilities for decoding emotions. Can you identify the emotion in this photo on the next page?

Getty Images

We want to understand what triggers an emotion—in ourselves as well as in other women. We know that we quickly react depending on the emotion we see displayed, such as in the above photograph, and we try to understand why she is feeling that way. Matsumoto, Frank, and Hwang (2013) help us:

1. **Label** our feelings as specific emotions.
2. Figure out the **trigger** for a particular emotion.
3. Identify which **nonverbal cues** we use to display these feelings and emotions.

The Emotion	The Trigger (what starts it)	The Nonverbal (what it looks like)
Happiness	√ Accomplished a goal.	√ Crinkled eyes (crow's feet). √ Big smile. √ Teeth showing. √ Eyes wide. √ Open body postures.
Anger	√ Injustice. √ Goal obstruction. √ Perceived violation.	√ Scowling face. √ Clenched fists. √ Reddened skin.

(continued on next page)

The Emotion	The Trigger (what starts it)	The Nonverbal (what it looks like)
Sadness	√ Loss.	√ Lowered corners of the mouth. √ Eyes down. √ Drooping shoulders. √ Closed body posture. √ Raised inner corners of the brows.
Disgust	√ Offended. √ Contaminated, rotten objects. √ Offensive persons.	√ Wrinkling the nose. √ Mouth/lip snarl (uneven). √ Shaking head.
Fear	√ Threat to our physical or emotional well-being.	√ Physically moving away. √ Stretched horizontal lips. √ Wide eyes (see a lot of the white parts). √ Brows drawn together.
Surprise	√ Something suddenly new.	√ Raised brows and upper eyelids. √ Dropping the jaw.
Contempt	√ Actions we consider immoral. √ Perception that person or action is below him/her.	√ Tightened lip corner or smile.

Many basic emotions we display (encode) and understand (decode) originate nonverbally in our faces. These facial expressions help us understand other's communication signals and emotional states. They are also intimately linked to motives, or intentions. Emotional expressions help us "read" each other—even without verbal confirmation or explanation. We seek to identify or make sense of other people's feelings, which is also known as empathy. We must also show empathy for other women, knowing how it will be received. Other women want to see empathy nonverbally displayed from us, as well.

"More empathic individuals may have increased emotional contagion, self-other processing, and theory of mind decoding when viewing emotional stimuli," according to Kana and Travers

(2012). So, when we encounter an emotional female, our emotional responses are triggered as we try to understand her intentions, desires, and belief systems. We constantly try to predict how she will act and react. Therefore, it makes sense that the more empathic we are, the more we will be invested in her emotional well-being—we'll even see it on her face.

Courtesy of Eye for Ebony

Empathy is seeing with the eyes of another, listening with the ears of another, and feeling with the heart of another.

—Anonymous

CHAPTER 3

Mastering Men's Body Language

Reading a man's body language often comes as second nature for both women and men. There's biology in this process.

"Men and women are believed to engage in behaviors that maintain inequalities present in society" (Smith et al., 2011). We know that strides have been made for gender equality and treating each gender with respect; however, these are no simple tasks.

Compared to men, women are often more sensitive when it comes to being on the receiving side of nonverbal communication. Women notice more nonverbals and may be quicker at processing cues. Regardless, the literature says that this "female advantage" helps with natural selection and social norms. A woman's sensitivity to innately help and care for others may actually require her to be more careful overall. Therefore, women's nonverbal actions are easier to read, and different than those of men.

"Men have more dominant personalities than women and hold strong experiences for the emergence of hierarchies than women do," according to Hall et al. (2008). When a task is framed as masculine or as a competition, men appear to be more motivated to succeed. The thinking behind this is that when a man is motivated, he pays more attention to nonverbal cues. Therefore, he'll have increased knowledge. Needless to say, all of us are more tuned in when we are motivated.

"Manly" emotions are used to "describe a type of highly controlled emotional expressions that has a highly expression norm" (Hess, 2016). Men often prefer to be in control of themselves whereas women, for the most part, do not like controlled emotions. We are more emotionally expressive. Hess (2016) has identified two reasons for these gender differences—status and social rules. Depending on one's social status, gender nonverbals differ. For example, think about work and two emotions, smiling and crying. Sometimes, a boss will actually smile at a lower ranking employee, confirming power and rank–almost seeming to enjoy the ranking hierarchy. Feeling some discomfort, the subordinate may actually cry to subtly confirm submission. And, let's face it, women cry more. Our societal rules state that men aren't supposed to cry.

Chun et al. (2012) find a difference in crying depending on who is around—we have a stronger emotional reaction when someone of the opposite sex is crying. Feelings of empathy from the opposite sex partner are evidenced in the research. And generally speaking, women cry more than men as a way to cope. Knowing that men do not cry as much, when men do cry, participants have faster reactions than when females are crying. When women see men cry, we have a strong need to attend to them. In crying situations, women may be better at displaying empathy and emotional support than men.

Beyond crying, society also tells us how to dress, act, behave, and think based on gender. Even when roles are gender-neutral, we assign male or female terms to them. English language pronouns clearly default nouns as feminine, masculine, or neutral. We use "him" or "her" without even thinking about it. You call for a plumber—you expect a man to arrive. You need a babysitter? No doubt a woman will watch your children. Society even channels professional work titles into work categories. For example, men are doctors; women are nurses. "When a profession is arbitrarily assigned to men, it's perceived as more

Credit: Oregon DOT, www.flickr.com

credible," according to Doering and Thebaud (2017). While these categorizations are breaking down, they still persist in significant ways.

Numerous communication studies ingrain in us the "social meanings of language, facial expressions, gestures, and body motion" (Epstein, 1986). And many argue that it's either biologically or socially-based. Regardless, determining these social meanings start in childhood.

WHEN I GROW UP, I WANT TO BE

As boys grow, they "welcome bodily changes, viewing them as evidence of muscular development rather than as signs they are becoming fat," according to Stephens, Hill, and Hanson (1994). Knowing that these inner feelings and perceptions are tied to depression and body image, boys and young men may be less afflicted than women. The language coming from their bodies—nonverbally, verbally, and psychologically—in many ways, prepares them better for adulthood, relationships, and communication.

Male body image starts in childhood—as it does for females. Boys, adolescent males, and men also suffer with body dissatisfaction. Studies find that, overall, they desire more muscular bodies. To achieve this, unhealthy male behaviors include maladaptive eating, compulsive exercising, and steroid use. One-third of boys go on diets to lose weight according to Watson et al. (2011). Yet, cultural standards for men are more flexible than for women. Men and women do not have the same experiences in terms of social expectations, perceptions, and body images. Men are more hopeful and less critical of themselves in terms of appearance.

During adolescence, a critical time for physical and emotional development, gender specific nonverbals take hold, and practicing intentional communication with one's body language begins. Boys notice girls, and girls start to engage with boys. Social interactions change. Feelings emerge and are displayed through nonverbal cues. Several nonverbals shed light on gender-assigned expectations. Starting in school, boys and girls have opportunities to practice their nonverbals and polish them. With time and practice, specific gender nonverbals mature for each gender.

Smiling	
Male	He smiles when he feels especially happy or friendly. Or when he needs to accentuate a specific point in speech.
Female	She is expected to smile more. In infancy, a baby who smiles more often is thought to be a girl and a baby who displayed negative facial expressions is labeled a boy.

Eye Contact	
Male	When a situation is positive, he will decrease his eye contact for a period of time. When he stops making eye contact, he is not likely to be interrupted during small group interactions.
Female	She maintains significantly more eye contact. When a situation is positive, she will increase her eye contact for a period of time. Her eye contact may help decode the other person's body language and nonverbals. When she stops making eye contact, she is more likely to be interrupted by a male during small group interactions. She may be deemed vulnerable when she doesn't make eye contact.

Kinesics	
(Body Movements)	
Male	When sitting, he tends to keep his back on the chair, but not his buttocks. This may look like slouching. He spreads his legs when sitting and standing. He consumes more physical space. He uses firm wrist actions when moving his hands and arms. Arm movement originates from his shoulders.
Female	When sitting, she keeps her back and buttocks close to the back of the chair. She keeps her legs together—even when crossing the knees or ankles. She consumes less physical space. Bent or broken wrist actions are perceived as a feminine nonverbal. Arm movement originates from her elbows.

Proxemics	
(Use of space)	
Male	He consumes more physical space. He does not like another man to approach closer. When he sits at the head of the table in mixed-gender settings, he is seen as the leader.
Female	She consumes less physical space. She allows both genders to approach closer. When she sits at the head of the table in mixed-gender settings, she is not seen as the leader.

Decoding	
(Interpreting nonverbals)	
Male	He is less accurate in decoding emotions. He is able to better recognize male anger. He struggles more reading facial expressions overall.
Female	She is more accurate in decoding emotions. Her facial expressions, overall, are easier to read. She is more adept reading facial expressions overall.

As women, when we display typically male nonverbal behaviors, a string of negative outcomes result (Spangler, (1995). Specifically, we are:

1. Perceived *negatively* compared to a man who exhibits the same behaviors.
2. Perceived to have *other male-dominant* characteristics.
3. Diagnosed as *needing psychological help* and counseling more than a man who displays these characteristics.
4. Judged to have had these problems *originate in child-hood*; whereas a man tends to have these issues only as an adult.

Those are harsh perceptions that pit traditionally male and female nonverbal expectations against each other. Interestingly, when men display feminine characteristics, they are not judged to be different than females, according to Spangler (1995). Meaning, a woman who uses masculine behaviors is "judged more harshly," but men are not judged to the same degree. If a woman isn't smiling, she is "perceived as less happy, less carefree, and less relaxed."

The accuracy in which we are able to process cues and behaviors in another person is called interpersonal sensitivity. These social perceptions can be gender-based and include the belief that women are more interpersonally sensitive than men. This also includes nonverbal sensitivity specific to men's abilities to read body language and nonverbal cues. Studies find that, most of the time, women are better than men at judging nonverbal tasks and cues—especially with facial expressions, vocal clues, and body movements. Compared to men, women report that they are more willing to express their emotions and disclose information. They perceive expressing their emotions "more often and more intensely than men" (Hall and Mast, 2008).

Other positive and impactful nonverbal displays include tilting the head up to project pride and smiling with the zygomaticus facial muscles (near the upper cheek and eye) to increase feelings of enjoyment and authentic happiness. On the other hand, hunching over elicits feelings of depression or sadness.

The way that men and women face each other within a physical space is a study of interest with varying findings. A summary (Knofler and Imhof, 2007) of gender-based physical interactions finds that:

→ Women prefer to face each other directly when speaking.
→ Men like to talk "at an angle" versus straight on.
→ Women will engage with a stranger if they are across from them.
→ Men, when talking with strangers, prefer to be adjacent (near or next to them).
→ Women will talk with female friends in adjacent or close positions.

Irrespective of how women and men face each other, engage, and communicate, our physical bodies speak a language for how we feel inside. Outside displays of inside feelings are real and should not be brushed aside. In terms of nonverbal cues and reading each other's body language, little is missed. It's a big deal.

MAN IN THE MIRROR

Men often believe that their body size is comparable to the size they think women will "like best" according to experts. Whereas women, in general, feel that men see them differently than they see themselves. Women who feel that their size does not align with the male ideal exhibit lower self-esteem and poorer body image, as discussed in Chapters 1 and 2.

Still, some men are not as confident in their perceptions of size and what they think women want. Men are divided—roughly half don't know what their partner prefers. In terms of self-labeling, however, more men than women say that their body size and the ideal aren't "far off." They feel pretty good about themselves overall.

Still, men desire an athletic body; specifically, they see the lean and muscular body type as ideal.

One study of black and white men's preferences for female shapes and sizes find specific differences. Overstreet et al. (2010) posit that black men consider larger female body size more attractive and prefer women with curvaceous lower body shapes. They also state that black men like a larger and voluptuous body shape over a thin or slender frame. White men, on the other hand, favor slim feminine body types. Both black and white men share a preference for "normal" or underweight body types as the best body shape for women.

Courtesy of Clarke Sanders

Women also have preferences for male body shapes. Sell, Lukazsweski, and Townsley (2017) posit that upper body strength is a big clue to a man's formidability. Over seventy percent of the 160 women surveyed said that physical strength determines bodily attractiveness. Being tall and lean are important. Sell and others aren't surprised that women find "physically strong men attractive . . . what did surprise us was just how powerful the effect was. Our data could not find even a single woman who prefers weaker or feminine male bodies."

A *Men's Health* magazine study (January 2, 2019) about the "ideal male body type" finds that women are attracted to:

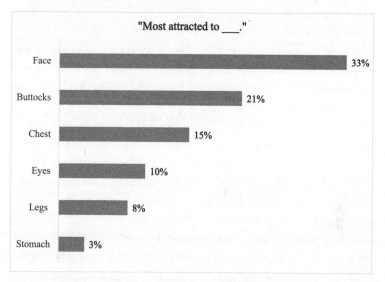

Men's faces take the top ranking when it comes to attracting women. We know the power of facial expressions, so it makes sense that being attracted to a particular face is due in part to reading its nonverbal expressiveness. Just in case you are curious, blue eye color (35%), brown hair (42%), and fair skin tone (35%) are ranked as the most desirable body traits for men in addition to being six feet tall with a thirty-three inch waist.

Getty Images

Women also notice and remember others' nonverbal behaviors better than men. They remember "dynamic cues such as shrugging, smiling, gazing, nodding, licking lips, touching hair, and gesticulating better than men" did (Hall and Mast, 2008). Women, compared to men, also recall others' appearance better—perhaps because of a documented "heightened interest" in clothing and appearance. I'm sure you can remember what the man was wearing in the last photo—or not wearing!

Each of us use our facial expressions and body to influence others and focus their attention. Whether we are sending or receiving nonverbal information, nonverbals influence how we evaluate each other. High power nonverbals communicate confidence, dominance, and assertiveness. For example, when men clench their fists, this increases how they feel about their power-related traits (Carney, et al., 2010). On the other hand, low power nonverbals present as smaller and result in fewer bodily displays. This makes sense in that our bodies expand and contract in relationship to our emotions and thoughts.

How men and women display power and dominance may have more to do with physical alpha displays and body chemicals than we think. Carney et al. (2010) tie this to evolutionary selection and hormones. We know that strong or powerful people engage with others and take more risks. Testosterone is directly related to increasing dominant behaviors and, in turn, dominant behaviors influence testosterone. It's a cyclical process in which one reinforces the other.

The hormone testosterone spikes as we ready for competition and drops when we experience defeat. Cortisol, a stress hormone, is also tied to power and behavior. It ebbs and flows depending on real or perceived situations. When expansive and powerful nonverbal displays are projected (such as sprawling or consuming a lot of space), research finds that testosterone levels increase while cortisol (stress) hormones dip. Meaning, by putting our bodies in certain "power pose" positions, our physical, logical, chemical, and behaviors shift to "feeling powerful" with increased risk tolerances.

"Cultural stereotypes depict men as more physically aggressive and women as more relationally aggressive" (Lloyd et al., 2018). Men are labeled by their physicality and women by their power in relationships. Specific to our brains, the male amygdala shows stronger activation and a tendency to react when the male individual sees cues of aggression—real or perceived. These feelings strike men's basic needs and they react. From sadness and hurt to anger and confusion, the "clear and direct expression of one's emotions is of upmost importance for meeting one's needs and promoting adaptive interpersonal functioning" (Mongrain and Vettese, 2003).

When women are ambivalent (have mixed feelings) toward men, we reduce our body language. Conflict carries a lot of weight in the emotion department and we must be diligent when it comes to expressing ourselves—both nonverbally and verbally. The power of emotions and feelings enables us to communicate messages toward another person regardless of being good or bad.

As women seek to express themselves, the "fear of consequences" pulls them back. "This conflict can manifest itself for both positive and negative emotional states and is distinct from the non-expression of emotion" (Mongrain and Vettese, 2003). As women, we question if we should say or do something that will draw attention to us—or remain quiet.

There is a relationship between conflict and emotional expression, with a high likelihood that negative outcomes will ensue from discord. From marital issues to low feelings of self-esteem, how we communicate during conflicts is important to understand and control. No doubt we want the freedom to express ourselves and often feel relieved and validated after we disclose our thoughts and feelings. For men, the freedom of expression has larger social boundaries compared to women.

BOYS WILL BE BOYS; SOME MEN WILL BE MENACING

Some male "bad behaviors" start in childhood, when boys do not feel liked. During this critical development period, evidence confirms that boys spiral down and act out as a result of not being liked by their peers. Of course, other factors like parenting styles and discipline play a part, but the literature suggests that boys who struggle to be liked have low social performance. They are likely to act out or misbehave as they get older.

"Sexism subtly influences social interactions to maintain the status quo of gender inequality" (Goh and Hall, 2015). Of course, we see gender differences and have some knowledge about the definition of sexism, but let's dive deeper. Typically, we hear sexism as it is related to discrimination or stereotyping women; many of us have either personally experienced it or seen it in action during mixed gender social interactions. I am encouraged to report that the perceived discrimination towards women has decreased over the past six decades, but it is still "rearing its ugly head" in both professional and personal settings.

Goh and Hall (2015) define two specific types of sexism: hostile and benevolent. Each has unique characteristics that include nonverbal cues, behaviors, expectations, and roles for both men and women. Hostile sexism is the "traditional" one that most think of when we see it in action. It's a dislike or misogyny towards women that "seeks to justify men's power in society through dominance and derogation of women" (Goh and Hall, 2015). Hostile sexists will berate or belittle—typically subjugating women—and is extremely negative in nature. This is typically not acceptable to women—and some men. Case in point, I once overheard a hostile sexist make a comment about his secretary's (not administrative assistant) body after she returned from maternity leave—saying that she hadn't quite got her figure back yet.

Harassment, a branch of sexism, often is associated with men's nonverbal expressions or displays towards women. Experts find that more extreme male harassers display more direct eye contact and whole body engagement towards women. Even a sly glance down her blouse is offensive, even though no words are uttered. There are definitive nonverbal actions with sexists' mindsets. And these are typically expressed through nonverbal (and verbal) behaviors and actions. We'll travel this route in the next section of this chapter.

The second type of sexism is benevolent sexism. Let me preface this with the fact that there is a big difference between being polite and well-mannered with the right intentions—and being a benevolent sexist. This subtly dangerous type looks like chivalry, as men position women in a seemingly harmless and positive light. We are portrayed as pure and warm, yet helpless and incompetent beings, who require cherished protection. This may even look like paternalistic affection. For example, does a man open the door for you because he's polite . . . or because he thinks that he's more competent than you? Does he insist on paying for your meal because he presumes that he makes more money than you? Does he think you need this pampering to feel better about yourself? Perhaps he feels like your protector because you need it. Does he carry the box for you, but really just wants to follow and ogle your backside? Remember, he looks innocent enough, but his mind and motivations may be rather guilty.

It's fairly normal that women can be attracted to benevolent sexism because of its allure. With this type of sexism, we are held in high regard—almost placed on a pedestal. These benevolent men appear willing to sacrifice and protect us; they may even "save" us. However, the root of this is not pure. And his words reinforce his desire to help "his little lady." This type of man perceives women as

Credit: Rydale Clothing (CC BY 2.0)

the "weaker gender" and his nonverbals, mindset, and words reinforce this.

Benevolent sexism is wrapped in an appealing package. Patience, smiling, feelings of warmth, and positive word choices with supporting affiliative nonverbals make this type of sexism attractive. Yet, there's just something "off" about the degree of patience, timing of the smile, extension of warm feelings, and double-edged word choices. When benevolent sexism is displayed or uttered in a room full of people, observers may pick up on it quicker than the target. This type of sexism is a stronger predictor of nonverbal impressions compared to when hostile sexist verbal statements often seen and heard. I recently attended a social in which the host, a man, turned to a woman nearby and pointed to a coffee pot. He then gestured to others' cups suggesting that she refill them. He then asked if she made the cookies on the buffet table. What? Can't men pour coffee and bake?

The subtle form of benevolent sexism is covert and influential. Sadly, this display of sexism can actually foster and reinforce gender inequality. Basically, "these supposed gestures of good faith may entice women to accept the status quo in society because sexism literally looks welcoming, appealing, and harmless" (Goh and Hall, 2015).

Benevolent sexism is sneaky and, by that, I mean in a gradual, subtle way, but with lasting, harmful effects. Compared to hostile sexism, this type supports the status quo. A woman will be heard "a little less" and treated with "kid gloves" because it is assumed she can't handle it. Interestingly, the research confirms that women overestimate the negative impact of hostile sexism while underestimating the harmful outcomes of benevolent sexism when comparing real-world experiences.

While individuals have overall positive attitudes towards women, women are consistently underrepresented in various professional domains, including C-suite roles and board positions. Along with this, women, compared to men, start with lower salary offers and are frequently given less financial and support resources.

Yet, verbal praise is offered to women for doing a great job or "being fantastic," which advocates an imbalance of gender, value, and treatment.

We definitely know the feelings that come from holding back unexpressed emotions, physically withdrawing, and, basically, shutting down during contentious situations. If stressful situations ensue without opportunities to communicate how we feel, "emotional experiences themselves become thwarted and lead to maladaptive secondary emotions, such as depression and distress" (Mongrain and Vettese, 2003).

CATCALLS AND COMPLIMENTS

"Secretly, all women like it when you catcall them," according to the mayor of Buenos Aires, Maricio Macri (di Gennaro and Ritschel, 2019). And, of course, "There's nothing more that a woman loves to hear is than how pretty she is." Please! We know this is not the case and many of us consider these so-called complimentary behaviors harassment.

Let's first define catcalls as "the use of crude language, verbal expression, and nonverbal expressions that takes place in public areas such as streets, sidewalks, or bus stops" (O'Leary, 2016). Catcalls also include "name calling, propositioning, wolf whistles, or comments evaluating physical appearance." Specific to nonverbal displays, typical actions include "leers, winks, physical gestures, and the use of signs to rate physical appearance . . . and, making a whistle, shout, or comment of sexual nature to someone passing by." You get it.

Ask yourself, why are these run-of-the-mill interactions important for us to understand—really understand—particularly for women? Think back to Chapter 1 and how we develop body image and self-esteem. Judgments on our appearance are challenging enough without a group of guys holding up six, eight, or nine fingers to assign us a value. These actions, solely based on appearance, are "particularly insidious because these types of verbal (and nonverbal) exchanges are *seemingly* innocuous and pervasive within westernized societies," says di Gennaro and others (2019). We even hear some say, "What, it's no big deal. She likes it."

Sadly, some women do perceive these as "compliments,"as long as appearance references don't turn too sexual. However, these appearance-based compliments violate expectations and healthy norms of behavior. Meaning, these types of comments are normally reserved for friends and family members, not complete strangers—let alone in professional settings. No doubt we've all witnessed cat-calling. The female target quickens her pace to escape, averts her eyes, and holds her bag a little tighter as a barrier of protection. We can almost feel her anxiety ramping up through facial expressions and body movements.

A 1969 *Glamour* magazine quiz, aptly titled "Do you act like a beauty?" even guides how women should respond to "walking along the street and a workman whistles appreciatively at you." Do you:

A. Ignore him.
B. Tell him he's being pretty fresh.
C. Call a cop.
D. Smile in a friendly acknowledgment and keep walking.

Such decisions! What should we do? *Glamour* says the correct answer is "D." "Women are told to accept a man's verbal or non-verbal behavior as complimentary without giving them a choice to interpret the behavior as an inappropriate intrusion into a woman's space" (O'Leary, 2016). You may have been taught that "A" is the right way to handle this situation. However, this comes with risks, as well in that "even ignoring catcalls can lead to their escalation."

Interestingly, there are distinct patterns based on gender, compliments, and catcalls—also known as harassment. Men tend to be complimented based on a topic, word choice, and status. For women, compliments come from a variety of sources typically associated with social norms and expectations. When a compliment goes from just that, a nonsexual specific word or gesture of praise or admiration, to the objectification of women—rewarding them for looking good—then harassment is in play—perhaps sexual harassment, as well.

These damaging actions coming from unknown men are termed "stranger harassment" and are simply bad. As to why some men do this, one study finds that "girl watching" serves three purposes:

1. It builds male camaraderie (bonding function).
2. It reinforces masculine identity.
3. It combats boredom.

Boredom—really? As though women are around solely for entertainment.

Ritschel and di Gennaro's (2019) interviews of more than two hundred women finds a "significant correlation between women's experiences with stranger harassment and increased self-objectification, a marginal correlation between stranger harassment and fear of rape, and a negligible correlation with women's reported restriction of movement." While not all attention is considered unwanted from men according to women, another study says that "sexual harassment" in many cases is "in the eye of the beholder" and that context matters." While "fear of rape" may sound a bit extreme, I ask: where does edgy nonverbal and verbal communication originate? At what point does it go too far? We tend to ask ourselves these questions "after" the fact. When do sincere compliments turn into unwanted catcalls?

If you're still not sure of what constitutes a catcall or a compliment, this chart provides a clear distinction of the features that are shared or specific to either compliment or catcall. The primary receivers of verbal and nonverbal display are women, and men are typically the senders. Therefore, this chart is based on typical "he sends, and she receives" information. I do want to clarify, though, that catcalling and harassment do occur from women towards men, but not to the same degree and are not received the same way.

Situation	Compliment	Catcall
She usually tries to "ignore" the remark.		✓
Includes nonverbal interactions like whistling or gestures.		✓
Man interacts with a woman.		✓
Interactions from a stranger in public places.		✓
She often interprets the remark as "offensive."		✓
Primarily focuses on her appearance.	✓	✓
Expresses his "favorable judgment" about her.	✓	✓
She feels judged.	✓	✓
She feels embarrassed.	✓	✓
She may feel threatened.	✓	✓
He usually acknowledges the remark (nonverbal or verbal).	✓	
Focuses on her performance.	✓	
Woman interacts with another woman.	✓	

Some of these situations are hard to distinguish between compliments or catcalls. We all feel judged, embarrassed, and threatened at times regardless of who is talking to us. And, how we accept a compliment about our new hairstyle may be completely complimentary on the part of the sender. There is ambiguity as to how offensive and respectful comments and gestures towards women will be received. We must be aware of the extreme possibility that actions could be misinterpreted. What are one's intentions? What does that wink really mean?

Men do not have the liberty of complimenting women they do not know; this quickly turns to stranger harassment and men should not be naïve. Remember, "We have to be careful about making assumptions about what women can or cannot, will or should do in a given context based upon demographic information. Instead, use a rich assessment of the situation when we are evaluating whether harassment occurred" (Gennaro and Ritschel, 2019). Men better think about what they are doing, who they are doing it to, and how this person (typically a woman) will take it—knowing that the odds are against it going well.

Specific to compliments, they are usually given in two distinct settings. In goal-oriented settings, compliments focus on a person's performance, ability, and skill. In unstructured settings, the focus of compliments is typically about daily appearance. Rees-Miller (2011) posits that the men and women do not compliment each other the same. Same-sex compliment topics are different than mixed gender compliments.

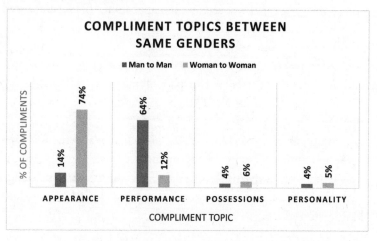

Overall, in goal-oriented settings like work or meetings, both men and women give and receive compliments at the same rate. In these settings, performance compliments are most frequent—as they should be, given the sensitive nature of this type of communication between people. Men also use performance compliments about sports in unstructured settings. We should not be surprised. But, the underlying reason for this may be tied to reinforcing each other's heterosexual masculinity.

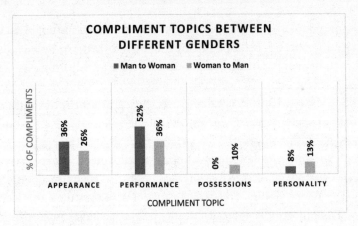

COMPLIMENT TOPICS BETWEEN DIFFERENT GENDERS

■ Man to Woman　■ Woman to Man

Y-axis: % OF COMPLIMENTS

COMPLIMENT TOPIC	Man to Woman	Woman to Man
APPEARANCE	36%	26%
PERFORMANCE	52%	36%
POSSESSIONS	0%	10%
PERSONALITY	8%	13%

While we think that saying something as "innocent" as a compliment based on appearance does no harm, our nonverbal reactions and feelings do not support this. Women are notorious for complimenting other women on their appearance (74%) compared to performance (12%). May I suggest, "You look confident." Or, "Great energy!" But not, "You look pretty," or "You look young."

Furthermore, there is a body of literature that talks about men and appearance. In fact, it is a part of men's overall well-being. Meaning, men do care about their appearance and who notices. However, it is un-masculine in our society to talk about male grooming and daily personal appearance. It tends to feminize the compliment when a man talks about another man's appearance. As a society, "what it means to be a man" has specific ways of "doing, making, evaluating, and speaking" (Rees-Miller, 2011) with four basic assumptions:

Assumption 1: At a core level, men and women are biologically and behaviorally different.

Assumption 2: To be a man means to be heterosexual.

Assumption 3: A man should be strong, authoritative, and in control (in contrast with women and other men).

Assumption 4: There are male bonds of solidarity, and men need to do things together without women.

Therefore, it is assumed that men talking about another man's appearance violates assumption one. And appearance compliments are typically feminine, thereby, violating assumption two. Thus, men should not compliment men on their appearance. Regardless, all of this unwritten and unspoken nonverbal communication makes us feel (and think). Perhaps the next time you compliment a woman, consider if you would bestow the same compliment on a man. I recommend that you take the gender out of the comment or compliment.

BODIES, BRAINS, AND BEHAVIORS

Gender differences are also evident in brain activation. One decoding strategy indicates that men analyze motor (physical movement) states more than women. Male brains, compared to female brains, show activity in the left hemisphere when the subject is judging another person's emotional state. For females, the right brain is activated more when analyzing intentions. Basically, our brains use different areas based on our gender and what we are trying to decode or figure out—including reading others' emotions, body language, and intentions.

Different parts of our brains are activated by body language, including our own and others' genders and personalities, as well as how we interpret emotions. Men use the right side of the brain when viewing emotional faces, scenes, and words. Whereas women's left brains are stimulated when looking at something they do not like or find to be emotionally aversive. Kana and Travers' (2012) conjecture that men have significantly greater left brain activation when judging physical actions (body movements), but female brains are not activated that same way—as evidenced by fMRI (brain scan) images. Basically, different parts of our brains light up (are more active) based on what we see and feel—and the brains of men and women are different. But you probably already knew that!

We use subtle visual and spatial cues to figure things and people out. Posture, gestures, and other body movements play a significant role in communication. For example, postural cues can show relaxed versus tense feelings and tired versus energetic feelings just by how we display our bodies. Leaning back or in with the torso can also convey different meanings depending on the situation. We are also drawn to or away from someone partially based on watching how someone's torso moves. For instance, when I cannot see the movements of hips, waist, and shoulders (trunk), it's hard to decode body language. We are also able to figure out biological sex and social dimensions, like personality, happiness, and power, through these body movements (Bahns et al., 2016).

"The process of person perception is likely to be faster and more efficient when it is facilitated by nonverbal cues" (Bahns et al., 2016). Their experiment on reading body language, specifically the torso, placed black bags over the torso area to hide the information coming from these body parts. After a series of perception experiments, they find that, without being able to see someone's torso, it is a challenge to understand attitude, behavior, and personality specifics. "When information from the torso is removed, functionality in social perception is substantially degraded." While the experts did not dive into specific cues like torso size, hip-to-waist ratios, or subtle trunk movements, they did confirm that receivers struggle to decode nonverbal information without a visual of the other person's midsection. Therefore, this is considered a "critical feature," specific to perceptions and communication. When the torso is absent from view, social interactions are impacted. We want to read this grand component of our bodies.

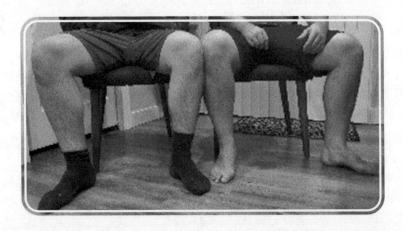

One component of male body language that does not require input from the torso involves men's preferred leg positions (see photo on previous page). Specific to gender, expectations, and stereotypes, men will "man spread" as a sign of superiority—displaying a wide-stretched body posture with open legs. This is indicative of power, as well as comfort. In advertising, men are usually filmed or photographed with their legs apart, regardless of whether they are standing or sitting. A lot of advertising has women laying down, sitting, or squatting. This is not the case for men who are rarely captured laying down. I ask you, could this be a sign of superiority versus inferiority with a subtle nonverbal postural display? Let's hope not. Images like this one are often sexualized as many eyes examine the crotch area, as the woman is posed with her legs open.

Getty Images

Interpersonal distance, the physical distance between two people needed for them to feel comfortable during a social interaction, reveals that women require less space to feel at ease. As part of our often natural communal roles, having closer bodily contact aligns with a closer environment. The data shows that people prefer smaller distances as a part of communal sharing. Women also sit closer to each other compared to men. Feelings of affiliation (bonded with others) may explain why distance impacts the sexes differently.

Not surprisingly, "individuals prefer larger interpersonal distance from individuals who are strangers compared to individuals who they know. Also, they prefer to keep a smaller distance with individuals who are younger than them compared to older ones" (Peker, Booth, and Eke, 2018).

When things are going well, we compliment other people more and make longer eye contact, as well. Our open body posture leans in and is receptive to other people. Yet, stressed individuals "experience ego-depletion and a failure to self-regulate that leads to [negative] behaviors," according to Lewandowski and others (2014). Stress and relationships are serious business.

STRESS AND THE SEXES

We all experience stress, and let's face it, stress impacts men and women differently. Under stressful conditions, people do not behave the same and this can harm our relationships. "Those who experience greater life stress have more negative interactions in their relationships" (Lewandowski, Mattingly, and Pedreiro, 2014). This is not surprising.

In terms of nonverbal communication, how we "see" stress in another person oozes through our vocal and body channels (93 percent +/-) much more than through our verbal (word) channel (7 percent +/-), as evidenced by infamous Albert Mehrabian's pioneering work on communication channels. Stress makes us do things that can hurt our relationships and ourselves. It changes the quality of how we communicate and comes through our body behaviors. The impact of stress on behaviors, bodies, brains, and relationships leads to a host of detrimental outcomes.

When we are stressed, we need to do something about it and, often, we will try to calm ourselves with small, self-soothing behaviors and actions. We touch our bodies (self-touch) as a way to comfort ourselves during stressful, anxious situations. "This is one of the most unconscious movements that we make," according to Eggert (2012). For instance, we may rub our hands together for comfort or chew on our lower lip as a way to calm our internal feelings of anxiety.

According to the American Psychological Association, "men aren't as likely to report emotional and physical symptoms of stress" (Santos-Longhurt, 2018). The evidence also suggests that men are "more likely to withdraw socially when stressed" and women, overall, manage it better.

Navarro (2008) and other experts offer several nonverbal behaviors related to stress. Some are specific to each gender and some are displayed by both men and women.

Men:
More robust self-touching behaviors.
Touching his face.
Stroking or rubbing the back of his neck.
Pulling the shirt collar away from the neck.
Preening (adjust his tie or suit coat).

Women:
Touching her hair.
Covering her suprasternal notch (soft area at the
neck between the collarbones at the neck base).
Playing with her necklace.
If pregnant, holding her stomach.
Ventilating her blouse to cool herself.

Both genders:
Exhaling slowly through puffed cheeks to slow breathing.
Rubbing the forehead or temples.
Drumming fingers on a surface.
Yawning more.
Crossing arms to hug self.
Whistling.
Scratching the forearms or other parts of the upper body.
Licking the lips.

Chewing gum faster.
Rubbing the hands back and forth on the thighs.
Squeezing the bridge of the nose while closing the eyes.

Lancaster (2001) differentiates coping mechanisms between men and women. For example, after a stressful day at work, "the typical man will respond one of two ways—by wanting to be left alone, or by taking it out on his wife or children." In contrast, a woman will deal with the difficulties of the day by "focusing on her children." To intentionally address this for people with children, I propose that fathers engage with the kids while mothers focus on a physical non-gender prescribed task. Dads change diapers and make dinner while moms mow the lawn or wash the car.

Regardless, we know that stress rears its ugly head through our bodies and behaviors and hurts both ourselves and those around us if not managed well. Our relationships will either suffer or soar based on how we use our body language.

Courtesy of Priscilla Du Preez

When the eyes say one thing, and the tongue another, a practiced man relies on the language of the first.

—Ralph Waldo Emerson

CHAPTER 4

Family and Friends' Body Language

Fierce loyalties and unwavering commitments to our family and friends are closely tied to the nonverbals our bodies share with one another.

Two are better than one. This saying has a lot of relevance in terms of time spent with others and the emotional payoffs for us. Research even shows that brain-to-brain coupling shapes our social relationships and behaviors. Several activities require another person, such as dating or working a machine, and cooperation and collaboration between two people are based on a set of unwritten rules and expectations. Between the sender and the receiver, our behaviors must be coordinated, and this usually involves our senses or feelings. The development of joint behaviors is "strongly influenced by interactions with other group members" (Hasson et al., 2012). Those interactions, of course, include nonverbals.

Childhood activities bond us to family members, from physical closeness paired with ample eye contact to having our basic needs met through food, touch, and time spent with caregivers. As we develop, playing games is one way to solicit cooperation. As well, several games require nonverbal mastery. "Rock, paper, scissors" and charades are two examples that depend upon nonverbals. Research confirms that these type of nonverbal interactions between people are quick and efficient—and effective. We understand these unspoken cues and respond accordingly.

Primarily, our visual and auditory (seeing and hearing) senses enable us to understand what is going on with the other person. Simply "watching a speaker's face is the equivalent of turning up the volume by fifteen decibels" (Hasson et al., 2012). Once our brains are "coupled" to each other via signals, we quickly and accurately exchange information. Often, this interactive alignment process is unconscious. It's called being in sync.

Our brains also "couple" with each other through nonverbal hand gestures and facial expressions. In one study, during a game of charades, fMRI brain imaging finds that temporal activity visually "carries information about the temporal variation" (Hasson et al., 2012) to the other person's brain. This means that mirror neuron systems detect the two network collaborations during social perceptions. Our brains, without speaking, code-share specific emotional information between the sender and receiver. That's intense—just for a game of charades!

Take another activity in which people will align with each other without speaking—perhaps rocking in a chair. Without really thinking about it, we begin to synchronize our rocking patterns. Walking next to someone may evoke the same unspoken nonverbal behaviors in that our gaits will begin to harmonize—perhaps even standing with similarly crossed legs and mirrored arm patterns.

Cialdini's (2007) classroom experiment highlights that we are drawn to others like ourselves. This makes sense for when we are part of a family unit. However, as we age and move beyond living with caring family members, getting others to cooperate with us may not always be an easy path. In our childhoods, school, playground, and social situations are ripe for competition rather than cooperation. Elliot Aronson's words in Cialdini's research explain how our emotions are dismissed during a classroom situation. This foundational process lays the groundwork for how we address some situations as adults

Picture a classroom filled with children vying for their teacher's attention. A few students are eager to answer the teacher's question and have their name called out loud. Compare this to some children labeled "shy" or "invisible" who drop their eyes and shrink in their desks. These students cringe at the thought of their names being uttered. As arms jut into the air for some seeking the teacher's attention, think about what happens after one child is called upon. Dismay and disappointment are "written all over" the other students' faces. As Aronson shares,

> This game is fiercely competitive, and the stakes are high, because the kids are competing for the love and approval of one of the two or three most important people in their world. In turn, this guarantees that the children will not like to learn and understand each other.

I urge you to think back to your own experience. Were you the eager youth with dancing eyes and a wiggly body in your desk? Did you take risks to answer the teacher's questions, or were you fearful of not knowing the answers? Regardless, this childhood competitive process starts early and, all too often, we fail to admire those risk takers. Rather, negativity or resentment prevail as we compare ourselves to others.

I'm not telling you anything you don't know when I say that sometimes situations are ripe for competition rather than cooperation. In every interaction with another person, our non-verbal displays demonstrate how we feel and how others perceive us. Genetically and fundamentally speaking, though, family relationships help stabilize cooperation and promote inclusiveness. Family members may "foster altruistic impulses and cooperative exchanges with individuals displaying those cues" (Christakis and Fowler, 2014).

Bunnell et al. (2012) posit that we consider friendship as an interpersonal relationship because it is quite different from blood or romantic relationships. Friendship "seeks out each other's company, exhibits mutually helping behavior, and is joined by links of mutual generosity and trust that go beyond those expected between blood and romantic." These bonds might actually be stronger than blood or romantic links! I challenge you to think of your best friend or closest confidant. What is your bond? Could you truly describe it and, if so, how does it differ from other relationships?

When we interact with friends and family, sometimes we become embarrassed, perhaps due to recalling a shared memory or breaking a behavioral norm. This social emotion usually happens when we are around other people, but is not often expressed when we are alone. In the company of friends and family, our embarrassment is usually less intense than when we around strangers or new people (Costa et al., 2001). Friendships and family relationships are not always consistently maintained. For example, you can "fire" a friend, but your family will typically remain close to you to some degree.

Nonverbals which demonstrate embarrassment typically include looking away, gaze aversion, disturbances in speech, face touching, silly smiles, and rigid posture. A fake smile in place of a real (Duchenne) smile while also looking down and touching one's face might be a typical look for someone who feels embarrassed.

Credit: Lindsey Turner (CC BY 2.0)

We display embarrassment nonverbals depending on the specific situation. Costa et al. (2001) point out five specific reasons or perceptions as to why we may feel embarrassed:

1. **Social evaluation:** We perceive that our actions are mismatched with our social identity—*That's not really who I am. Please don't exclude me from the group for what I did.*
2. **Awkward interaction:** We fail to behave according to social scripts and rules—*I didn't mean to trip and fall. Honestly, I only had one drink.*
3. **Loss of self-esteem:** We believe we fail our own personal standards—*I'm known for not losing my temper, and I can't believe I yelled at her in front of everyone.*
4. **Corrective action:** We want to recommit to social norms and prompt forgiveness—*I humbly apologize for putting my hands on you when you asked me not to touch you.*

5. **Appeasement**: We display submissive or affiliative behaviors because we violated a rule—*Let me make this up to you. I'm shocked at my own behavior.*

As you see, each of these conditions includes someone else, thereby confirming that embarrassment is specific to social conditions and is not usually experienced when we are alone.

However, observations made by Costa et al. (2001) of nonverbal displays found that they happen in general whether we are alone or with someone else. When we are alone, the following nonverbal displays occur from most frequent to least frequent:

1. We move our lips.
2. We shift our gaze.
3. We rotate in a chair.
4. We touch our face.
5. We gaze down.

When we are with others, more shame, embarrassment, and anxiety result. In the company of someone else, the order slightly shifts.

1. We move our lips.
2. We rotate in our chair.
3. We incline our head.
4. We move our hands.
5. We shift our gaze.

While moving our lips happens regardless of the situation, when we are embarrassed around someone else, moving in our chair comforts us (being cradled) if we are sitting, and using our hands makes us feel secure—like we feel in childhood with trusted family members.

The intensity of our facial expressions may also be less extreme when others are present compared to when we are alone. We try to "save face" or have a "poker face" rather than letting our feelings of embarrassment show on our faces. Around others, there is also a decrease in the number of body movements, hand movements, and vocal cues. Being able to control one's self around people is a social expectation. Evidence suggests that men do not feel embarrassed as much as women do. Yet, we all remember those situations and unpleasant feelings.

PINKY PROMISES

"Friendship, through its entanglements with relations to power, may cast light on important expressions of being human in terms of individual emotional and social and cultural well-being" (Bunnell et al., 2012). How we engage with our friends and family members not only conveys information, but also influences behaviors. This is human nature, and nonverbals significantly enhance interpersonal relationships. Thus, we should master nonverbal communication to improve our friendships. When we successfully interpret clues, cues, codes, and signals, we are then able to enhance how we communicate and interact with the people in our lives.

Close relationships and appreciation are important aspects of communication. When we want to be polite, we present positive facial expressions to others. We are quite sensitive to friends and family members who sometimes fail to appreciate what we do for them. Often, our sour facial expressions give us away. Too often, "negative relational outcomes" are the result of failing to show our appreciation to someone. To ensure that our friendship nonverbal behaviors are supportive, we spend time together as a means of expressing appreciation. As we forge bonds, we align our social beliefs through the concept of "affiliative social tuning." We unconsciously adjust our own social nonverbal cues to align with others in our group.

Nonverbal codes based on Gheorghita's (2012) work include:

Performance codes:	Body movements, facial expressions, glancing, touching, and tone of voice.
Spatial-temporal codes:	Use of time and space.

| **Artifact codes:** | The meaning of objects in communication. |
| **Mediating codes**: | Special conditions between two people interacting with each other. |

Sometimes we think we are sending clear messages, but something still goes amiss. All too often, we overestimate the clarity and intensity of our own expressions. Biases also change how nonverbals messages are decoded. Case in point, you accidentally catch two women glancing your way and you immediately think, "they are judging me"—and it's negative. This is not always the case. However, we often fail to gather additional information for clarity—and our hurt feelings prevail.

Carton et al. (1999) found that poor relationship quality impacts overall well-being. Specifically, inadequate or ineffective nonverbal skills negatively impact our interpersonal relationships.

Courtesy of Hian Oliveira

Persons with healthy, positive relationships most likely have greater opportunities to improve their nonverbal skills (with partner affirmations), thereby resulting in more satisfying relationships.

While some experts believe that appreciation is a "taken-for-granted" aspect of friendships and family dynamics, others highlight the importance of being emotionally strategic with appreciative actions. Two characteristics of friendship, based on expert findings, state that friends are "less concerned for things like giving and receiving" (Bello et al., 2010), but want gratitude acknowledged. A nonverbal expression of gratitude and touch might look like an eager handshake or hug.

When we live our ordinary daily lives with little conflict, everyday nonverbals and emotions are ambiguous, weak, and unclear. There is little need to be intentional or on guard. We are comforted with relevant information, social contexts, cultural rules, and predictable knowledge about our family and friends. Our calm internal state is subtly expressed through our emotions. When we engage with someone we like, we will synchronize with her or him—mirroring or copying each other's body language. For example, we might lean in and laugh at the same time as our friends or family members. From afar, this may look like a "dance" of some sort in that our bodies and behaviors are in sync.

The lack of nonverbal mimicry can also provide us with vital social information. "Direct gaze interaction has been identified as an important moderator of mimicry" and "averted gaze has been shown to facilitate and intensify the perception of fear expressions," according to Bruder et al. (2012). Fear, as most of us know, seeks direct communication routes to connect with another person.

We are social animals who seek to interact with others. As we express ourselves through our facial and body movements, we are also picking up on the patterns of our family and friends. These patterns are called dispositions—the need to quickly understand what someone is doing and react appropriately. We must make quick and accurate judgments.

When we engage with a friend or family member, we mimic or coordinate our posture, gestures, facial expressions, and mannerisms. Our simultaneous actions reinforce interpersonal communication and bond us. There are many payoffs for performing these often unconscious behaviors:

- Feelings of being connected
- Better cooperation
- Compassion
- Warmth

Depending on the nature of the relationship, emotional mimicry serves as a social regulator. We use our emotions and nonverbal actions to express our intentions and attain our goals—through both cooperation and competition. Often, we react to someone with specific facial expressions. We are extremely sensitive to facial expressions in that we measure "very subtle expressions which are only barely visible" (Hess, 2016). These displays tell us what the other person is thinking or feeling, and contribute to our desire to create social warmth. We also know that if we don't have good feelings towards another person, we will not mimic their actions.

Most social situations are predictable and ritualized. Saying hello, goodbye, and asking niceties require little cognitive or emotional thought. A host of cultural ceremonies, like family dinners or celebrating a friend's birthday, gives us plenty of opportunities to nonverbally communicate with predictable patterns and reactions. We count on this control over our environment in order to regulate our stress levels. People adapt quickly and, as needed, pay close attention to body language. "We are wired to attend to appearance cues and behavior that can signal threat on one hand or cooperation on the other" (Patterson, 2017).

SO MUCH COMMOTION OVER OUR EMOTIONS

When we set out into the world, we transmit information about ourselves to other people. From clothing to posture, information about our personality and feelings seeps through both our nonverbal and verbal displays. When we see certain postural cues, we associate them with openness, dominance, affiliation, or submissiveness. For example, when we move towards someone whose arms are open, we quickly see this as a welcoming gesture. If we see closed arms across the chest then we are instantly aware that this person is not "open" to us—and we want to know why and wonder if there's reason for concern.

Social fear reduces feelings of well-being and decreases our engagment with peers, for both men and women. Women, more than men, have higher levels of social anxiety (Blasi et al., 2015). Often, these feelings center on our bodies, both reflecting our perceptions of our body image and displaying our discomfort with a situation through physical means. However, when younger adults, in particular, have strong peer groups, these negative feelings are lower and positive friendship qualities increase. "It can be argued that social context becomes a determining factor in many everyday interactions" (Hess, 2016). Blasi et al. (2015) also find that those with higher levels of education and professional goals show higher levels of social anxiety. Both pressure on one's self and peer pressure can lead to debilitating mental and physical outcomes.

Different social contexts or environments also impact how we read each other. Think of your comfort level while spending time with your friends at someone's home versus out at a restaurant or bar. Norms and expectations vary from person to person with hidden rules and expectations for most interactions. As an example, extraversion can be expressed through personal styling and neat clothing. Conscientiousness has been linked to formal attire, and narcissism may be revealed through expensive or flashy clothing choices (Bahns et al., 2016).

In theory, social processes affirm that our emotions are intimately connected to each other. Barrett (1993) posits that emotions are developed and communicated in specific ways:

Emotion-relevant movements	• These movements communicate emotions internally, behaviorally, and/or socially. Our movements are based on relevant actions and reactions depending on the sender and receiver.
Emotions are viewed as members of "families of emotions."	• Emotions share crucial characteristics that help us predict, understand, and change them, as needed.
Facial movements are only one of many forms of communication of emotion, rather than having special status as *the* clear-cut indicators of emotion.	• While facial expressions do reveal emotions and provide a lot of information about our emotions, we should also consider body actions and vocalization patterns. Touching, changes in skin color, and postural shifts are just a few non-facial movements for understanding someone's emotions.
Communicating emotions is always embedded in context.	• There are no movements that can be considered clear-cut, context-free expressions of emotion. We must consider emotions in different contexts in that, without taking in the whole situation, we are unable to fully and accurately understand that emotion.
Socialization plays a crucial role in the development of emotions and communication.	• Our society has "feeling rules" regarding which emotions are appropriate in social situations.
There are many emotional and non-emotional influences for communication behavior, and this has important implications for emotional clarity and accuracy.	• When a situation is clear-cut and well-understood, it is easy to understand emotions; however, in complex, natural situations, a more fine-grained approach may be required to process interactions.

How we communicate is key for developing emotionally healthy friendships. This communication can be dependent on the display of both conscious and subconscious emotions, as well as our nonverbal responses overriding what we might verbalize.

Nonverbal information carries information about social group membership, and we tend to apply stereotypical knowledge associated with a person's group. For example, if our friend is wearing glasses, we will probably judge her as more intelligent, dependable, industrious, and honest (Kuster, Krumhuber, and Hess, 2019). We will also try to figure out her intentions, thoughts, and behaviors through her personal grooming, including choice of clothing, hairstyle, and scents. We do not need much time to make these judgments. For some appraisals, less than a second is enough.

Communication is affected by more than just another person's body language. From the temperature of a room to the dimness of the lights, we pick up on environmental cues and adjust our own nonverbals too. For instance, did you know that pleasant smells increase our likelihood of helping others? (Patterson, 2017). And soundscape cues of noisy crowds and overwhelming screams cause us to have negative judgments. We will physically retract in order to avoid unpleasant conditions.

Sometimes we infer a particular occupation and gender when we look at a person's clothing. Nonverbal clothing cues impact how we judge someone and are not always dependent on reality. For example, if you see someone wearing scrubs walk into your local coffee shop, you instantly think that he or she is in the medical field. It's the uniform. This is true for several types of clothing—lab coats, jeans, shorts and flip flops, and ball gowns—based on when and where we believe they should be worn.

Although we look at appearances to decode people, facial expressions help us process and understand thoughts and behaviors to an even greater degree. We are strongly influenced by emotional body language as well. Carton et al. (1999) research on nonverbal skills and relationship success find that the ability to decode facial expressions is linked to peer rejection or acceptance. As we navigate our world, we continuously send and receive signals validating and verifying us within it. Fortunately, friendships make the journey better as we seek acceptance from others.

PLANTING THE SEEDS

Female friendships are extremely influential for the cultivation of nonverbal communication and vice versa. In childhood, girls who have trouble with identifying emotions have fewer female friendships and more male friendships in adulthood. "Girls who have more male friends at the beginning of high school may have difficulty making friends with girls. These 'male-friendly' girls may be viewed as being odd, different, or a threat by other girls. Such perceptions may be difficult to change" (Rowsell et al., 2014).

Courtesy of Yanapi Senaud

Girls appear to have higher-quality friendships than boys during development, although both genders have equal levels of inherent enjoyment developing friendships. In turn, these important relationships set the foundation for adult intimacy. Childhood friendships are beneficial in that they teach us to help each other and reinforce our self-esteem. However, caution for young relationships is warranted because "bad" influencers may contribute to bad behaviors. And, sometimes, these young friends, or mean girls, bully or pick on each other as a part of childish actions and attempts to navigate social acceptance.

When we struggle to identify other's emotions, our overall well-being is impacted. Experts confirm that having positive social relationships are essential for overall well-being and health. "Friendships are some of the most important relationships" and having at least one friend impacts "development, adjustment, and buffering against loneliness and social dissatisfaction" (Rowsell et al., 2014). Self-esteem also spikes when we have friends. Friends help us with collaboration, perspective, empathy, and looking to the future. It's important to learn how to establish healthy (for the right reasons) friendships.

Friendships are considered the most common form of social relationships. When people struggle to develop friends because of their emotional skill level, their self-esteem and social quality are negatively impacted. Females who are emotionally aware have more friendships compared to males as a whole. This may be due in part to women's need for social networks. We like to hang out with people we resemble. To some degree, genes have a role in the formation of friendships, and we pick people who have traits and behaviors like us. Remarkably, Christakis and Fowler (2014) posit that "pairs of friends are, on average, as genetically similar to one another as fourth cousins." Really? Being human not only involves our physical and biological environment, it also includes our social environment. And, not surprisingly, women like to talk more and be emotionally engaged at higher rates than men.

Courtesy of Ben White

Male friendships tend to be more superficial and less intimate, according to the research. Men prefer to have structured activities and be active when interacting with their friends. They also tend to talk less about themselves and share fewer emotions compared to female friendships. Sometimes we find it easier to hang out with men in part because of these factors. Additionally, friendship is not a substitute for romantic love, but viewed as a model of intimacy for many. Sometimes the word friend includes everyone from casual acquaintances to those with whom we have very intimate relationships.

The health of a friendship is a factor in how the relationship grows or struggles. When women are distrusting, suspicious, and cynical, we are more apt to exploit or manipulate our friends. This relational aggressive is actually common among female friends and seen as socially acceptable behaviors—through gossiping, rumors, and excluding certain people. Sadly, as we know, peers will support these damaging actions in that they trust their female friends and see these behaviors as bonding.

Spending time together and sharing information are two key features of strong friendships. Interestingly, when friends spend time with other friends who are not part of the same group, attitudes can change, and this can benefit the group as a whole. Not surprisingly, studies find that out-group friendships can impact how other in-group friends feel about each other.

Davies et al., (2011) find that:

In an active, transactional friendship, where partners see each other often and frequently disclose information, more visual and verbal cues signaling group differences are likely to emerge over time, making group categories salient even as such close friendship experiences are also like to provide very personalized experiences of contact. Simply put, the more actual interactions that take place between cross-group friends (your "other" friends) over the course of the relationship, the more opportunities exist for friends both to be reminded of their differing group memberships as well as to learn that they are each unique individuals who may share some meaningful commonalities.

By having different friend sets, relationships may be strengthened and reinforced. Degrees of "closeness" vary and do not mean the same thing to each person.

Credit: Matthijs Strietman (CC BY 2.0)

On the other hand, frequent and subtle relational aggression negatively impacts female friend relationships. Women with high levels of distrust and cynicism "may exploit this norm of female friendship by seeking interactions and closeness in order to manipulate" (Abell et al., 2015). These same women report that their friends manipulate and question their trust as well. These types of Machiavellian behaviors also "reduce the need to feel emotionally close to another individual." Overall, these adults report low qualities of friendships. Obviously, these types of unhealthy relationships don't last—no one likes these people, and no one is content to prolong the friendship.

YOU'VE GOT A FRIEND IN ME

What does it mean to be liked? That's a tough question. According to dictionary.com, to be liked is defined as "having the same characteristics or qualities as," or being "in the same way." As an aspect of being liked, Buil, Hoot, and Lier (2017) posit that "time" and "touch" nonverbals are also factors. As we form social contacts, we judge and are judged by our behaviors. When others show "low social preference" for us, we may display poor behaviors as a result. In turn, we will not be liked by others. Case in point, I attended a social event and did not feel immediately welcomed by the group of men talking amongst themselves. I just stood there with my drink, waiting for them to give me their time, or at least make eye contact and nod. After a few minutes, another woman entered the room and walked directly towards me and we hugged. At no time did the other group show a preference for engaging with us. I wasn't impressed and this made a lasting impression on me.

We like people who are like us. Our personalities mesh. We share similar views, our lifestyles seem to gel, and we genuinely enjoy each other. This sets the tone for the beginning of an authentic friendship. How this relationship starts involves both nonverbal and verbal cues that give us affirmation that things are going well. We may like the same genre of music or be a member of the same club. Perhaps we live in the same dorm and attend English class together.

We "wish to be liked in order to increase our compliance and can accomplish that purpose by appearing similar in a wide variety of ways" (Cialdini, 2007). We might share backgrounds and interests that draw us together. "Wow, I have a brother, too." Or, "I don't like lima beans either." Perhaps she says that soccer is her favorite thing in the whole wide world as well. Whatever the topic, our likes and dislikes mesh well with those of other people who interest us. And our body language mimics this as a way to show interest. If she jumps up and down in delight, then we jump too. If she raises her hand for a high-five, then we high-five back. If she leans in really close to share a secret, then we lean in close to receive it. This "mirror and match" communication method draws us in.

"We are phenomenal suckers for flattery—we tend, as a rule, to believe praise and to like those who provide it . . . even when it is clearly false" (Cialdini, 2007). Ouch. Really? Yes, even when the claim or action isn't sincere or true, we are lured in.

We must be honest with ourselves about the authenticity of our friend relationships. What is it about our friend that draws us in and sustains us? The literature talks of the "scarcity principle" and how we hold onto certain things when we assign value to it. The scarcity principle is defined as "a limited supply of a good, coupled with a high demand for that good, that results in a mismatch between the desired supply and demand equilibrium. Theoretically, when there's less of something available, it creates a greater demand for that something" (Nelson, 2017). When we apply this to friendships, then our commitment, desire, and love are impacted. When there's a little of something, we hold on tighter and value it more. Perhaps this is why we have a "best" friend or two. We also hate to lose what we have. To explain this, the term "reactance theory" proposes that, when we believe that someone or something is being taken away, we feel unpleasant reactions.

Dr. Cialdini (2007) writes, "Impressive amounts of our behavior can be explained by examining the tendrils of psychological reactance. Before beginning such an examination, though, it would be helpful to know when people first show the desire to fight against restrictions of their freedoms." We want what we want—without restrictions or limits. And we count on our trusted friends to help us.

Our friends influence us, and these influential relationships have a host of benefits and costs depending on a few predictable factors. This is actually true for every social interaction, but when it comes to friends, our return on investment is really important. Marmaros and Sacerrdote (2006) offer a clever formula for determining an interaction with another person and how this interaction may or may not progress.

Information gathered + Shared experience benefit –
Time used = Degree of friendship

So, let's look at this a couple of ways. You meet a new person, chit chat, perhaps share a single experience, but then don't meet again—the odds are low that a friendship will develop. On the other hand, if you take the time to learn things about her, share a lot of meaningful experiences, this increases the chances that a relationship will develop. This is common sense. Information and experiences help us form friendships—really, any notable relationship. The cost of time, will not warrant such a loss of friendship when the other investments are ample. In other words, once you "know someone well, which raises 'information gathered' and 'shared experience benefits,' then it pays to continue to interact with that friend even if the friend moves far away ('time used')" (Marmaros and Sacerrdote, 2006).

How we meet our friends is important for the development of the relationship as well. Here's a list of factors that have positive effects on the likelihood that two strangers will interact:

Geographic closeness: Perhaps you sit by her in elementary school or live on the same street. As an adult, she's your office cubicle partner.

Family background: You share similar values and rules, like spending the night at each other's houses or sharing meals together. As adults, you talk often about the number of children you want to have and raising your kids together.

Common interests: You like the same band or, perhaps, go off to college together and join the same club. As an adult, she's your travel partner as you check off your bucket list.

Racial similarity: We hang out with people who look like us. Perhaps you attend a college with particular racial compositions. As adults, you both join a specific diverse professional association.

This isn't to say that your best friend necessarily grew out of a childhood friendship, or that you are both Latinas. Rather, the literature posits that a host of factors, including race, gender, and background, form friendships. "Geographic proximity and race are greater determinants of social interaction than are common interests or family background" (Marmaros and Sacerrdote, 2006). Regardless, "long-term friendships grow from chance meetings" and sharing experiences strengthens the relationship—even if you move away from each other in later years. Those "long-distance" friendships remain intact because the bonds developed early.

"Friendships are horizontal relationships between two peers who expect reciprocity in sharing the costs and benefits of mutual interaction. On average, friendships also enhance well-being in the face of stressful events" (Ojanen et al., 2010). With friends, we are able to express intimacy, receive validation, and have fun with little conflict. As Ojanen and others say, "the need for closeness is a fundamental human motivation."

How do we make a friend? The intrinsic (internal/inner) desire and extrinsic (external/outer) motivation to develop a friendship are at play in seeking these relationships. For some, we create a friendship based on joy and positive feelings. For others, the friendship may address external pressures or rewards. We do know that we are better off with friends than without them.

When we invest in a friendship for intrinsic reasons, the extrinsic payoffs are usually small. We know that being extrinsically motivated will diminish the quality of such a relationship. That "what's in it for me" attitude doesn't sit well. Intrinsically motivated friendships, on the other hand, are self-satisfying just by their composition. People who have friends for intrinsic reasons report that they benefit from the relationship by increased intimacy and having fun over time.

To better understand how we develop relationships through social interactions, Jaegher et al. (2010) offer a framework of its complexity. These complex interactions offer a mix of participants, different contexts, and unique nonverbal and verbal styles.

> They impose strict timing demands, involve recipro-
> cal and joint activity, exhibit a mixture of discrete and
> continuous events at different timescales, and are often
> robust against external disruptions.

Meaning, over time we develop special relationships with hundreds of individuals[en dash]each with their own sensory elements and unique characteristics. Individuals work diligently to stimulate others' senses and create memories, so contact is not lost. Sometimes it's what we remember about another person as it is imbedded in our memory.

You've heard about having baggage. We all have it, though we frequently associate it with unresolved issues or even childhood trauma. In terms of nonverbal communication, our baggage is part of our "biology, culture, gender, and personality" that we bring to social settings (Patterson, 2017). This shapes our behavior and has predictable outcomes. How we send and receive messages are interlaced with cues and clues from our personal baggage.

CONFIDANTS IN MY CORNER

The female friend relationship is known for being unrestrained and easy. Views are readily discussed, opinions are voiced, and "intellectual familiarity" is shared. When women spend time together and talk about their feelings and personal information, relationships grow stronger. Evidence even suggests that we "are able to distinguish friends from strangers based on blind odor tests," according to Christakis and Fowler (2014). When we smell things the same way, we understand that particular environment. Smell is linked to our emotions and communication processes.

"Women's female friendships are multi-leveled and longer lasting and have greater involvement than men's same-sex friendships" (Aleman, 1998). Through our same sex friend relationships, we dialogue without restraint and freely express our inner feelings. These mutually respected, caring, and trusting relationships are important for women. With same sex friendships, we are free to take emotional risks with comfort, and many find these relationships as places to rehearse "thinking" and intellectual play. With female friends, we are able to freely dream, challenge, and reflect—like unbridled thinking. Being around other women and nurturing these friendships yields emotional and intellectual payoffs.

Intellectual confidence is also developed between female friendships. Almen (1998) eloquently states, "Female friends nurture each other's intellectual and academic self-esteem through a partnership that provides an unintimidating stage on which to perform their thinking. Women friends are integral to each woman's authorship. Connected and bearing responsibility for a friend's growth, women friends teach each other and learn from each other without the tension brought about by individualistic objectives. Women friends reconcile the tension between interdependence and autonomy in such a way that learning becomes truly collaborative."

Authentic friendships also tend to be more fluid and less spatially bound once they are developed. They can also be short-lived or long-lasting—but all are a form of intimacy. Friendship may be considered a basic human need in that we desire human contact.

We give and take through our nonverbal (and verbal) conversations using two basic types of interaction styles: focused and unfocused. Patterson (2017) defines focused interactions as conversations that usually include words—though just by being physically close to someone, conversations of some sort usually happen. Focused interactions typically have verbal give-and-take patterns, including eye contact, to determine what adjustments are needed during exchange of information.

During conversations, women look at the other person more; it's more intense with longer continuous periods of time. When listening to others, women show a greater gaze time as compared to men. Men, however, interrupt eye contact more than women, which is attributed to more male body movements. A man may shift his body and expand his torso—making his body bigger. Or he may uncross his legs and cross them the other way. He may adjust his body in the chair. Usually, his movements are expansive.

Sometimes, focused interactions happen when we speak, and others only listen. In this case, our nonverbals support our message and include a myriad of predictable actions (Patterson, 2017):

1. An increase or decrease in **gesturing** that aligns with our verbal content.
2. A shift in our **vocal intonations**—usually including a drop in pitch near the end of our words.
3. **Decreased volume** when we come to the end of what we are saying.
4. **Long pauses** between our topic or monologue.
5. More **gazing** to ensure that our receiver is actively listening to us.

Additionally, our listener will also display nonverbal cues, including inhaling and exhaling, posture shifting, gestures, and higher volume (amplitude) when preparing to speak. Posture is a rich source of nonverbal information and helps us to understand what other people are feeling and, in turn, how to adjust our bodies to match.

Unfocused conversations, however, happen without words and include social situations—like standing in line at the bank or passing someone on the sidewalk. Have you ever sat and people-watched at the mall? No doubt you have watched a lot of unfocused interactions between people. With unfocused interactions, we position our bodies in relationship to other people, and express ourselves entirely using our nonverbals.

Mimicking happens through an array of emotions, from sadness and despair to happiness and delight. This social referencing starts early in life and relationships as we "seek out emotional information from a significant other person in our environment and use that information to make sense of an event that is otherwise ambiguous or beyond our own intrinsic appraisal capabilities" (Bruder et al., 2012). In other words, we look to another to judge a situation based on feelings of what makes sense. Specific to feelings and reading nonverbals, happiness, anger, and sadness are easy markers to help us understand what a woman needs. These expressions are potent and emotional signals quickly influence our friends' emotional reactions. This "autonomous feedback process" is rapid, subjective, and helps us make sense of what's happening right in front of us.

When friends get together, emotion-based communication happens without the need for a lot of thought. One person can easily impact the feelings, thoughts, actions, and reactions of their friend. Facial expressions are used to communicate with other people and often include social motives and personal needs. The research confirms that there is a "positive association between increasing degrees of sociality and the amount of people's smiling behaviors" (Bruder et al., 2012). We smile more when someone in front of us is there to receive it.

According to the experts, when we watch other people, our own motor planning is stimulated. As we try to figure out what the other person is doing, our decoding strategies kick in. For example, our

Getty Images

use of smiling impacts others' behaviors especially when we both find something funny and amusing. Smiling elicits affiliation as a binder while helping foster cooperation with others. Another emotion, fear, elicits mutually negative feelings from the other person and we tend to come together under the conditions of common threats including pain or loss.

Social appraising is the root of shared understanding—especially with our emotions. Defined as "perceiving others' emotional expressions . . . and, inferring underlying appraisals," this skill allows us to be empathetic and display appropriate nonverbals based on our feelings (Bruder et al., 2012). For example, open body posture increases our empathy while decreasing feelings of our dominance. Looking at someone's posture enables us to infer personal characteristics about her or him.

We mutually express intimate emotions and encourage the exchange of communication with our female friends. This "convergence in emotional responding increases as people grow closer to each other" (Bruder et al., 2012). For example, when we see a friend's sad expression, we move closer and interact. No words are required and our desire to offer comfort is immediate.

Friendship homophily has ramifications in that like-minded

friends gravitate towards each other and influence each other. So, it matters who we pick as our friends. Friends are considered special in that "contact over time and across many situations develops meaningful, close relationships under conditions that facilitate improved attitudes" (Davies et al., 2011). Friends share activities and self-disclose which assists in developing emotional bonds and trust. Feelings of closeness often sustain across long periods of time. And sometimes we are "two birds of a feather who stick together."

Courtesy of Nqobile Vundla

Confidence is not posting endless selfies, or repeatedly protesting how happy or in love we are, it's a subtle yet noticeable sheen that emanates from our being—our eyes, our words, our body language.

—Sam Owen

CHAPTER 5

The Powerful Body Language for Love

You're not quite sure why, but your body language, in the context of romance and love, is on high alert.

"Men are expected to take the lead in many social scenarios and interpersonal interactions involving both biological sexes" (Gulabovska and Leeson, 2014). In the romance department, research finds that women view their bodies as less ideal compared to how they believe their partners view them. In turn, this leads to lower self-esteem and negative body image for women, as discussed in Chapter 1.

In dating, appearance is the most frequent compliment topic, with personality as the second. No doubt, men focus and respond to physical attributes when judging women. "A social impression can be generated after a face is seen for only around 100 milliseconds" (Gao et al., 2017). Faces also influence the perceptions of what we see as masculine or feminine.

Without this visual communication, "People tend to exchange information at a slower rate while forming less accurate interpersonal impressions" (Kotlyar and Ariely, 2013). Suspicions arise when we cannot process and decode all streams of communication—both nonverbal and verbal. As the experts posit, "Women may be especially sensitive to the presence of nonverbal cues during online chats."

Using computer-generated avatars with online dating, Kotlyar and Ariely (2013) find that face-to-face communication and physical positioning provide "substantially better perceptions of each other, greater information disclosure, and enhanced desire to meet in real life." Women's perceptions of encounters are positively impacted when they can watch the body movements of the other person. By being able to observe the environment and the other person's movements, women are able to reduce their levels of ambiguity. Interestingly, men report more interest by just looking at a fixed (static) image without movements. When men watch the avatars' bodies move, they are actually less interested in pursuing a relationship. That may help us understand how visual men are in terms of interpreting still photographs without a lot of "noise" to cloud their cognitive processes.

When we start dating someone, it is wise to improve how we communicate with each other. However, add together online dating and the inability to decode nonverbal cues through limited visuals, and it becomes even more challenging to get to know someone. Text messaging, photograph editing, and subjective online profiles limit the opportunities for reading nonverbal cues. We want to see body movements, facial expressions, and background details to learn about the other person. Even the image below includes photos to help us decode the text—the images show smiling faces which reinforces their corresponding written messages.

With the goal of developing a relationship, many opt for online platforms. According to eHarmony, forty percent of American adults use online dating. However, the struggle for genuine connections is real. Online dating can fail to produce long-term, healthy relationships because of the importance of geography. "Where you live will impact your online dating experience simply because certain locations have more acting [online] users." And, sadly, both genders lie about their online profiles. eHarmony's research shows that twenty percent of women admit to using photos that make

Getty Images

them look "younger and thinner." For men, forty percent say they lie about their jobs "in an effort to sound more successful" (www.eharmony.com/online-dating-statistics).

Datingadvice.com even offers the "2019 Good, Bad, & Weird" of online dating:

1. Match.com has almost 24 million users.
2. Four percent of US marriages start from an eHarmony relationship.
3. Globally, there are more the 7,500 dating websites.
4. Roughly forty-nine million people have tried online dating.
5. Fifty-nine percent say that it's a good way to meet other people.
6. Two-thirds of online daters actually have gone out with someone with whom there was a match.
7. Gender ratios are about fifty-fifty.
8. Online dating is a $2.5 billion dollar annual revenue.

Additionally, it's interesting to see which age groups use online dating. Where are you?

Age	Percent
18–24	27 %
25–34	22 %
35–44	21 %
45–54	13 %
55–64	12 %
65+	3 %

Now, I am not saying that online platforms don't work, but I am suggesting that millions of honest communication efforts fail, along with heartbreaks and hookups, as a result of limited and questionable visual information. While text-based communication has a purpose, the absence of nonverbal cues also impedes match-making. Words are important, but are not our primary means of communication—tone and bodily clues are even more essential.

Knowing that a compliment involves verbal, vocal, and nonverbal cues, it's important to talk about flattery and dating. Studies show that when a man compliments a woman in a dating context, he usually targets her appearance. And women perceive the men who give these pleasantries as being more intelligent. Gao et al. (2017) suggest that complimenting a woman's appearance lets the woman know something about her "quality." This may be done via flirting, which often involves nonverbal behaviors like winking, mouth movements, gestures, and postural displays.

YOU MAKE ME FEEL ALRIGHT

Nonverbal communication is a significant part of how couples communicate and feel. These nonverbal messages define the state of one's relationship and are even known as "intimacy's primary vehicle" (Bernecker et al., 2018). Couples set two common types of relationship goals:

1. Approach relationship goals
2. Avoidance relationship goals

Approach goals focus on positive experiences; avoidance goals seek to avoid negative experiences in relationships. When nonverbals are coupled with these goals, they influence relationship satisfaction.

Plenty of research on relationship goals confirms that those who make sacrifices and use approach motivation have more positive emotions and greater satisfaction with fewer conflicts. The converse is true for negative avoidance experiences. Avoidance is linked to a person's increased sensitivity for signals of threat (Bernecker et al., 2018). Those who focus on approach relationship goals had more positive involvement with their partner. Those who exhibit avoidance relationship goals are tied to withdrawn and more negative involvement. Women who display avoidance goals may miss opportunities for creating positivity with their partners. Women who match their partner's positive behaviors display more satisfaction. Apparently, positivity pays off!

Specific body gestures also accompany positive emotions (Sauter, 2017). Some prosocial positive emotions are recognized in part by specific body language expressions.

Prosocial positive emotion	Body movement
Love (*commitment to intimate relationships*)	Head nods, Duchenne smiles, forward leans, mutual gaze, affiliative hand gestures, open posture, hugging, stroking, and full body movements. Fewer vocal signals, slower speech rate, low voice intensity, low pitch level and variability.
Compassion (*help in response to someone suffering*)	Forward leans, touch—patting and stroking movements.
Gratitude (*when someone helps us*)	Touch—primarily a handshake. Big smile.
Admiration (*seeing another's extraordinary achievement*)	Vocal exclamations. No recognizable body language.

Other nonverbals that increase positive emotions, called positive involvement behaviors, include eye contact, touch, body openness, leaning in, smiling, head nodding, and close space (proximity). Smiling, a strong social nonverbal, can trigger feelings of "affiliation, ingratiation, and positive effect" based on Hall et al.'s (2007) work. They also state that nodding helps us to regulate actions and interactions. Eye contact (gazing) is tied to our emotions and the use of hand gestures "facilitate smooth discussion and may reflect personality characteristics such as extraversion."

Head nodding is extensively studied and can have different meanings (Hall, 2006). Specifically, we use it to indicate understanding, agreement, desire for the other person to continue speaking, reassurance, or confirmation of what we hear. This little gesture has a big nonverbal role in communication depending on the sender's intent and the receiver's interpretation. Many studies, as well, conclude that nodding is only associated with lower status and submission without considering its role in relationship positivity.

Some nonverbal signals can have multiple meanings. Therefore, it is important that we "clarify which meaning or function is operative in a given situation and what the motivational correlates are" (Hall, 2006), in order to reduce misunderstandings.

Destructive negative avoidance withdrawal signals include avoiding eye contact, displaying closed body postures, and holding the head in down positions. It's important to gauge our use of eye aversion in that we might appear submissive—unless that's your intent. On the other hand, "sustained eye contact can make you appear confident and in control of a conversation" (Wilson, 2009).

Getty Images

Does being vulnerable have its own set of nonverbal cues? Book et al. (2013) find that men are "more likely to select 'submissive' women as potential victims" partially based on how they walk (gait). They state that the perception of dominance includes expansive gestures with arms and legs, including eye contact and big body postures. Specific to women's gait, those with "less synchronous" walks are viewed as less confident and more vulnerable. Vulnerability cues also include slower walking speed with shorter strides. While Book and other's work focuses on perceptions of vulnerability from a specific population of men, the fact that our walk plays into part of our nonverbal communication is important and, thus, we should be intentional about our gaits in social environments where we might feel threatened.

When we present a closed posture to our partner, this may signal a "reduction in the immediacy" between a couple (Meadors and Murray, 2014). Additionally, these actions are linked to anxiety, stress, and discomfort in both ourselves and in our partners. We will also self-touch in social situations in which we feel anxious. Women will physically soothe themselves more than men, which might include touching their face or arms more. This may also have something to do with self-consciousness or nervousness. During awkward situations, men will increase the frequency of posture shifts; and if they self-touch, it's usually on the upper part of their bodies or throats—or covering part of their face or holding their head.

Courtesy of Christian Erfurt

Postural positions can also signal interest and concern. A closed and rigid posture says "stay back" whereas an open and relaxed body posture is inviting. Examples of open body postures include widespread arms and open hands to indicate ease, compared to a closed posture that involves the arms wrapped around the torso or close to the body with closed palms conveys the opposite. The same holds true for leg positions—relaxed and widespread, or tucked closer to the hips for protection. Posture is also used for power and status. We associate gracefulness, awkwardness, clumsiness, and coordination with posture too. Those with a higher status tend to have a more relaxed posture around lower social status individuals.

Hall, Coats, and Smith-LeBeau (2005) point out that "a person low in power is dependent on those with more power in specific interactions." And the "less powerful person needs to please others by being pleasant, needs to attend to others' moods and desires by gazing at them, needs to be interpersonally sensitive in order to optimize interaction outcomes, and is expected to be deferent and polite by using constrained body movement, taking up less physical space, sitting up straight, and so forth." I think much is expected of the person who doesn't feel equal.

As biological creatures, our gender differences do not go unnoticed as we develop relationships and, frequently, express our sexual or romantic desires to be with another person. Williams (2013) notes that "men judge a woman's walk and dance significantly sexier when she is in the most fertile part of her menstrual cycle." How's that for body language! While this warrants caution in practical applications, we should know that at a biological level, our bodies emit odors and clues about us.

Reading your partner's nonverbal signals is a large part of how we communicate in relationships. We are especially sensitive to negative emotions. For example, when we see anger, it often looks like a lowering of the eyebrows with a square and tight mouth. Contempt or disgust may present as an asymmetrical (offset) mouth, lopsided smile, rising of the upper lip, or tightening of the corners of the mouth. An angry touch may include hitting, pinching, or squeezing another person to elicit a painful physical response. Feelings of anger are quickly associated with a higher status and men report experiencing and expressing anger more than women. If someone is disgusted with us, he or she may push or pull us through an aggressive touch.

Credit: Mark Stevenson (CC BY 2.0)

Fear may be seen as a horizontal stretching of the lips with raised and straight eyebrows. Kimberlee et al. (2004) note that deception also has signs of concealed emotions. Physically, we may experience a tremble if we feel fearful. When we see someone with threatening facial expressions, this may elicit fearful facial expressions from us as well as the related feelings. This is intensified when the body and gaze are directly positioned toward the receiver.

Experts confirm that relatively unhappy couples "tend to make greater errors in nonverbal communication" (Carton et al., 1999) compared to adjusted and happy couples. They find that people who are unaware of their poor nonverbal communication skills should proceed with caution. These difficulties could have both emotional and physical outcomes, including depression. Nonverbal communication conveys our inner thoughts and feelings—and they are quick to appear in opposite sex romantic relationships.

COME-HITHER LOOK

Did you realize that flirting has different styles? These include physical, traditional, sincere, polite, and playful. More than "100 nonverbal behaviors are thought to be indicative of romantic interest" (Hall and Xing, 2015). Being open to a relationship has its own set of nonverbal clues, including more smiling and an increased frequency of touching the other person. Signaling "openness" has dozens of nonverbal cues. Each flirting style has nonverbal cues and impacts courtship development. We use these nonverbals to show dominant, sincere, cautious, playful, and comfort behaviors.

Flirting Style	What It Feels Like	What It Looks Like
Physical	Level of comfort you feel using your physical body to express romantic interest.	Nods head often during initial contact. Glances flirtatiously. Shows open hands and palms while speaking. Does not touch one's self when talking to the other person.
Traditional	Men should make the first move and women should not pursue men.	Nods head often during initial contact. Men show open hands and palms near the end of the conversation. Women show hands and open displays for the entire interaction. Men lean in during the encounter. Men have higher pitch in their tone of voice. Men cross their legs less. Men nod their head more during the interaction.
Sincere	Showing emotions and sincere interest in the other person.	Does not touch one's self when talking. Women show more flirtatious glances. Women smile and laugh more. Men have a higher pitch in their tone of voice. Men cross their arms and legs less. Men lean in near the end of the conversation.

(continued on next page)

Flirting Style	What It Feels Like	What It Looks Like
Polite	Uses caution, proper manners, and is less forward.	Does not touch one's self when talking. Men nod more. Men are not physically close. Men do not tease.
Playful	Fun, self-esteem enhancing while acting playful.	Does not touch one's self when talking —in the beginning. Extends or protrudes the chest. Women have more flirtatious glances. Women shrug more. Men cross their legs less.

(Hall and Xing, 2015)

Additionally, the experts find that people who are attracted to each other tend to engage in less self-touch while displaying flirtatious glances during the start of interactions. Women are also more likely to smile and laugh at higher frequencies. Men tend to gaze (stare) more while crossing their legs less during the beginning of the interaction. Men also use higher pitched voices to indicate interest in the other person.

In the romance department, satisfaction and gratitude are connected. We all want to be appreciated. Bello et al. (2010) suggest that we display nonverbal behaviors like "giving assurances, sharing tasks, offering support, and displaying affection" as ways to confirm our appreciation for the other person. As well, people who are most open to casual sex will behave in certain ways to signal availability. Bellow et al. (2010) categorize nonverbal displays of appreciation that romantically-involved participants share:

Behavior or Feeling	Nonverbals
Physical affection	Hugging Kissing Holding hands Touching
Helpful	Helping actions like cooking, assisting with a project, etc.

(continued on next page)

Behavior or Feeling	Nonverbals
Emotional support	Listening Comfort through touch Leaning in Nodding head Eye contact
Sacrifice	Sharing time Physical investment (working hard), etc.

We all use various means and methods to express our feelings to our significant others. The research suggests that these person-specific expressions of helping and favoring our partner are the most important because they demonstrate our individual concern for our relationship.

With our partners, we notice and react to the other person's emotions—often called emotional contagion. This is defined as "the tendency to automatically mimic and synchronize expressions, vocalizations, postures, and movements with those of another person and, consequently, to converge emotionally" (Hess, 2016).

When we gaze at someone, our emotional intensity heightens. We want to see what our partner is looking at as we look at him or her. A wink. A glance. Playful eyes with raised brows. We evaluate eye contact along with facial expressions to determine value. "Gaze direction appears to not only influence emotion perception but does so through the process of direct perceptual integration and indirection attention capture" (Hess, 2016). Whether we stare with a longing look or bashfully bat our eyelashes when flirting, these nonverbal cues provide critical information in relationships.

Gazing is considered fundamentally important because we are visual beings and gather information about the other person when we watch, stare, glance, or gaze at him or her. Patterson (2017) points out that high levels of gazing are evident among couples. This fairly unconscious behavior happens when two people are seen holding hands; it's like a trance and we are captivated with the other person.

In less than one second, we are able to detect expressions in the face. "Facial expressions play an enormous role in understanding, tracking, and responding to the feelings of those we care most about" as Kimberlee et al. (2004) explain nonverbal expert Paul Ekman's work. Experts even suggest that facial displays are the "best predictors" of marital dissolution (divorce)! Their research accurately predicted divorce outcomes ninety-four percent of the time.

Credit: Guian Bolisay (CC BY-SA 2.0)

"Facial movements are the primary means of communicating emotions," according to differential emotions theory (Barrett, 1993). Studies link facial expressions with emotions and overall well-being. For example, perceived dominance is associated with facial expressions like anger, happiness, and fear. Smiling, on the other hand, is linked to impressions of affiliation—being relatable—because smiling is perceived as warm and welcoming. And, as we know, these appearance impressions stick with us for a long time.

Often, "We manage our facial expressions more than we do our other behaviors" (Patterson, 2017). Specific to happiness, "Women are assumed to experience and express happiness more than men in a variety of contexts (Hertenstein and Keltner, 2010). In reality, more women do report being happy compared to men, and we usually smile more too.

TALL, DARK, AND HANDSOME?

"As relationship intimacy increases, so does the typical level of nonverbal involvement between two partners" (Patterson, 2017). When we are looking for a mate, stereotypical preferences emerge. Specifically, men demonstrate a penchant for "younger, shapely females with symmetrical features, clear skin, and lively behaviors," according to Patterson's (2017) research. For women, a "somewhat taller, older, dominant-looking male with resources" may capture her attention.

From higher pitches to softer cooing with emotional inflection, how we linguistically engage with a potentially romantic partner is evident. Women vary their tone more than men and have a wider range of pitches. Men, on the other hand, tend to speak louder and not as fluently or smoothly—even though they may think they are quite smooth! Even though differences between the sexes may be subtle, our initial sexual behaviors may be tied to "power differentials" and, of course, are situation specific.

Sexual script theory argues that, "Men are traditionally the initiators and women the restrictors of sexual activity early in relationships" (Vannier and O'Sullivan, 2011). These gender-based roles prescribe that men pursue women. And, no surprise, the media often reinforces these sexual advances—from soap operas to steamy-hot dramas, men "hunt" for a desirable woman and "take charge of the sexual encounter."

When men are asked to imagine themselves in a sexual situation, many say that they find it easier

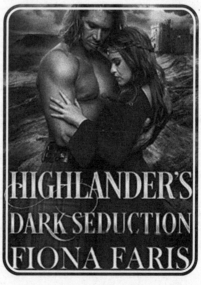

Credit: Johnnie Edwards (CC0 1.0)

to picture themselves initiating first contact than responding to a woman's contact. When women are asked about the "ideal or romantic sexual initiation scenario," they, too, envision their male sexual partner as the initiator (Vannier and O'Sullivan, 2011). However, women see themselves as the controller of the time and pacing of the interaction. Research confirms that men do, in fact, initiate sexual activity more often and women do initiate sexual activity depending on the length of the relationship, degree of feelings, and the situation.

One study finds that ninety-one percent of male-initiated sexual encounters are non-verbal invitations (compared to sixty-five percent verbal) or encounters. While sexual encounters frequently involve little verbiage, nonverbal communication varies based on age and experience. As young adults, men and women "begin to develop stronger, more meaningful relationships with their romantic partners" (Vannier and O'Sullivan, 2011) and whoever initiates sex may be important for later-in-life happiness. Younger adults count on nonverbal behaviors and actions to start sexual activity and, as the research points out, use fewer words during sexual acts though they were not totally silent.

Kissing and hugging are two nonverbal and indirect strategies that prompt sexual activity and are more common than direct asks. Subtle, indirect actions are more desirable and are more common than verbal statements. Vannier and O'Sullivan (2011) posit that individuals picture their sex lives easier by initiating through nonverbal means than verbal asks. In turn, these indirect and nonverbal actions are perceived as more natural and spontaneous and do not require verbal confirmation. When women want to initiate sex, they may use direct strategies to show a high degree of confidence that their message will be well-received. However, most opt for indirect nonverbal strategies to offset fears of rejection or coming on too strong.

In established, long-term relationships, more predictable and patterned activities are documented specific to sexual roles—from coy and clever to brave and bold. Older, established relationships appear to have greater freedom for either partner to initiate sex and display sexual nonverbals to demonstrate sexual interest. Ideally for most, long-term relationships would have sexual satisfaction as a part of their success formula. Blunt-Vinti, Jozkowski, and Hunt (2019) note that "increased communication between sexual partners is associated with higher levels of sexual satisfaction" for both men and women. On the other hand, casual or less committed relationships use more nonverbal strategies.

Both genders depend on nonverbal cues and clues during sexual encounters. Men tend to use hugging, kissing, and tickling. Women prefer to remove clothing, to fondle, and to touch their partner's genitals. Both genders are likely to respond similarly to their partner's initiations and they will match or mimic their partner's nonverbals. This synchrony (behavior matching) is persuasive and usually viewed as a positive way to align with each other. "When we're attracted to someone, studies show that we often begin to imitate their posture or movements . . . to reflect a positive affirmation of behavior" (Wilson, 2009). This subtle, yet impressive, nonverbal behavior may disarm the other person by putting them at ease.

For some, talking about sex is embarrassing and evokes insecurities. It could even ruin "the mood" if words overpower actions. Nonverbal communication is less awkward and threatening—and most opt for it. With a gentle guide of the hand or brush of the lips, these nonverbal cues "speak" more about wants and needs than verbal instructions. Many college-aged men state that they were are comfortable with nonverbal strategies for sexual consent. If they are rejected, they feel like they "save face" more so than when they are given a verbal rejection. Overall, facial expressions and body language may be less threatening than verbal barking or spoken rejections or demands.

Nonverbal messages are used both before sexual activity as a way to ask if the person is interested in a sexual encounter and during sexual activities. For example, putting on a condom does not require verbal directions and handing the package to the partner should be a self-explanatory nonverbal. Especially when accompanied by a coy glance and Cheshire cat grin.

When women verbally state what they want from their sexual partner, they may deviate from being the "passive gatekeeper" in traditional sex roles and expectations. Scholars (Vannier and O'Sullivan, 2011) say that it's "more acceptable to be silent" than give directions or state preferences. These should come from non-verbal actions and are likely to happen before and during sexual activities. I urge you to think about whether the scholars who study gender dynamics are correct. Remember that we are all unique women when it comes to sexuality—no apologies necessary.

Sexual satisfaction includes a couple's use of both nonverbal and verbal communication. Nonverbals are associated with more feelings of comfort through cues like facial expressions and non-verbal sounds (breathing hard, coos, sighs, etc.), instead of verbal statements. When couples share that they are sexually satisfied, this is related to positive nonverbal communication. When each person analyzes both their verbal and nonverbal communication activities, they find higher levels of sexual communication satisfaction and, in turn, increased sexual satisfaction. Remember:

1. More communication is better. Our nonverbal and verbal responses and, in particular, our partner's nonverbal responses confirm sexual communication satisfaction.
2. Sexual communication is a predictor of sexual satisfaction.
3. Communication is an important component not only of sex itself, but overall relationship satisfaction.

Communication is incredibly important. We are well-served to work on our sexual communication for establishing long-term payoffs for sexual and relationship satisfaction—with a focus on nonverbal communication before, during, and after sexual encounters. Too often the focus is on foreplay, yet the literature posits that communication during sex is vital for overall satisfaction and well-being. Those little touches and brushes with our bodies are noticed and important for humans.

REARING ITS UGLY HEAD

As Mongrain and Vettese (2003) point out, "Conflict over express-ing one's feelings could be expected to undermine the clarity of interpersonal communication and impair one's feelings of agency in relationships." In other words, conflict messes with how we commu-nicate and harms our relationships. You probably already know this.

You might have even had thoughts like, "I worry if I express negative emotions such as fear and anger, my partner will not approve of me." Or, "I'd like to show him how I feel, but some-thing seems to be holding me back."

Research on communication-related issues uses questions to understand feelings of intimacy, the need to self-protect, and outcomes around loss. Often, these questions and feelings rattle around in our brains and empower us to act—or paralyze us—lit-erally and emotionally. Yet, Mongrain and Vettese (2003) share that, "without a clear sense as to what we are feeling, highly ambiva-lent (mixed emotion) people [will] be expected to be less congruent in their expression and have difficulty communicating clearly and assertively in their relationships." Feelings of powerlessness and hopelessness are a real part of bad endings as many of us know from past or present relationships.

During conflict situations, the literature finds that, when women "hold back" their anger toward their partner, they restrict their nonverbal displays and may be passive or submissive toward their partner. There is an interesting relationship between conflict, nonverbal actions, fear, and self-expression. Specifically, when a woman has mixed feelings, including fear or worry, disapproval, or retaliation, she will show this through her nonverbal displays. While our words may be neutral or perhaps positive, our true feel-ings will "leak" through our body language—perhaps being phys-ically withdrawn, reserved, and void of natural facial expressions.

Of course, holding back emotions can damage any relation-ship, but is especially harmful in romantic relationships. "Women's absence of expressions of love is interpreted by their romantic part-ners as a hostile response" (Mongrain and Vettese, 2003). Hostile?

When we, as women, hold back our innate loving behaviors, this could play a crucial role in "escalating conflict within romantic relationships."

Courtesy of Ben White

Needless to say, this makes for muddy waters and can cause both parties to potentially lose. It's hard to interpret and express feelings as a part of crucial conversations. Sometimes we "read too much" into emotional displays—in particular, strong facial expressions and body movements. In the end, though, our relationships will struggle if we fail to address conflict through healthy nonverbals and verbals.

We know that ambivalent women silence themselves, which leads to both short-term and long-term negative outcomes. In the short run, the couple flails and argues, and in the long run, depression, self-worth, and withdrawal can occur. Both physical and physiological health are impacted. It's important to express thoughts and feelings through facial expressions, gestures, and other nonverbals in order to "get it out" and "be heard." Being heard does not mean screaming—it means communicating in such a way that both the sender and receiver accurately decode the messages. And this takes time to master.

Constructively expressing anger to establish healthy boundaries is important. Candid and assertive nonverbal and verbal messages convey emotions and thoughts. Expressing both negative and positive feelings are necessary for meeting our needs—both personally and professionally. Yet, we must always remember that negative consequences may result from unbridled displays of emotional expressions, as most of us know all too well.

Jealousy is an ugly emotion. We've most likely either been on the giving or receiving end of it—and usually with bad results either way. Relationships can become damaged, and jealousy can lead to extreme violence like murder and suicide. Regardless, this emotion has a front and center seat in many romantic relationships. This "protective mechanism" is defined as an "attitude of vigilant guarding against the threatened loss and an effort to preserve the status quo by maintaining possession" (Zandbergen and Brown, 2015). That may just be a fancy way of saying, "He/She is mine."

We also see a set of nonverbal cues linked to jealousy and the perception of threat. Different behaviors are exhibited from men and women through thoughts, emotions, and actions. Romantic jealousy is no different.

Oddly though, some see jealousy in a positive way in that they have a "feeling of commitment and confirmation for relationship stability" (Zandbergen and Brown, 2015). However, this still creates conflict and fights between couples. Sometimes, people will evoke jealousy to get an outcome they desire from their partner. For example, you catch your partner looking at another female and, instantly, your emotions leap into hyperdrive, which then signals to him to lean in and snuggle your neck to confirm that he's with you. One little look and we react.

Social media posts can also elicit jealousy. Four of the most common conditions that evoke emotion include infidelity, expectations of time and commitment, social media posts, and self-esteem. Zandbergen and Brown (2015) note that women are "significantly more jealous to emotional infidelity" than men. And both men and women feel about the same regarding sexual infidelity. I urge you to think about your displays of jealousy and what prompted these. How did you react? Were you out of control with your body displays? Are your reactions predictable?

Nonverbal patterns emerge from negative situations, too. We are familiar with verbal bullets shooting our way during an argument, but nonverbals also fire. Specifically, angry people may move very close to the other person while staring and waving their hands wildly. We instinctively and immediately know that we do not like this type of body language.

Anger and physical aggression are correlated—and detrimental for a relationship. Not surprisingly, women report that they are "less satisfied" (to say the least) when physical and psychological aggression are exhibited by their partners (Hettrick and O'Leary, 2007). From adolescense into adulthood, aggression is documented from both males and females. Interestingly though, "female aggression is more socially accepted than male aggression" and women's "physical aggression has less severe consequences" compared to men. It's alarming, in any case, that our bodies and these behaviors are present in any relationships.

Specifically, women report that they push, grab, and shove during physical encounters. Male aggression is seen as intimidating and enticing fear in their female partners. Most relational aggressiveness stems from anger and temperament, not self-defense. Not surprisingly, these relationships have lower levels of satisfaction and positive feelings toward their physically aggressive partners.

While relationship violence tends to start in mid-adolescence, it may continue into adult relationships if not addressed. The research (Hettrick and O'Leary, 2007) suggests that youth conduct problems and antisocial behaviors are later associated with aggression and bad physical behaviors. And, "arguments in adult intimate relationships almost always precede physical aggression."

Wives report that anger and coercion from their husbands are why they engage in mild levels of physical outbursts. Experts posit that "controlling behavior and jealous behavior in dating relationships are predictive of physical aggression of both males and females" and we need to talk about these negative, horrific displays of nonverbals to communicate our internal feelings. During disagreements, "the person initiating a topic of disagreement is more likely to touch in order to try and influence the other person to agree with his or her position" (Smith et al., 2011).

"Power in a romantic relationship is often based on the perception that one has the right to make a decision," according to dyadic power theory (Smith et al., 2011). Power, the ability to act and possess influence, influences one's partner in marital situations. Couples exert their power either individually or collectively to get what each want. If one feels that a part of the relationship is unresolved or out of balance, he or she may touch the other to influence and ascertain agreement. The nonverbal gesture of touching increases compliance. If touch is used to make a request, we are more likely to comply. During conflict, touch often exposes true feelings and overrides verbiage.

As well, we use touch as a nonverbal for intimacy and power. It has the power to communicate "anger, fear, disgust, love, gratitude, and sympathy" (Hess, 2016) and many of us are familiar with these feelings that stem from being touched. Hess (2016) also finds that a "squeezing touch" communicates "unpleasant and aroused emotional intention" compared to a "finger touch" which communicates "pleasant and relaxed emotional intention."

When arguing, wives display more dominant behaviors than their husbands. Interestingly, Smith et al. (2011) posit that spouses differ in their use of touch and that most touching happens when wives chose the topic for discussion. Meaning, under different circumstances, wives may display more domineering behaviors, including touch, to strategically influence their husbands. Wives also use more hand touches than husbands regardless of the topic. But, when husbands chose the topic for discussion, touching behaviors do not vary. Perhaps we see touching as an easy way to help our partners understand us. And we know that touch has healing benefits, as well.

TOUCH AND GO

"Men appear to initiate touch more than females" (Hertenstein and Keltner, 2010), but more women "perceive a touch as sexual." When touch is used by strangers, like at a nightclub for example, women perceive touch as cool and unfriendly. Men, on the other hand, view a strange woman's touch as "warm, pleasant, and friendly." "There are a host of sexual [nonverbal] cues which are neither anatomical nor physiological, but presentational" (Epstein, 1986). From stance to eye movements and lip licking to hand gestures, when individuals are sexually interested, nonverbal displays kick into gear. Both genders display these to gather information and progress the interaction. Some suggest that women initiate touch first, but others think that the behavior is more typical of men. Regardless, the meaning of touch and its nonverbal implications are important.

Touch is "associated with intimacy and positive effect" and couples report to have "better psychological well-being," according to Debrot et al. (2013). We communicate with our partner when we touch him or her.

"Hugs by the husband are linked to lower blood pressure and higher oxytocin levels" for couples. (Debrot et al., 2013) and just by holding our partner's hand, stress-buffering effects happen. Touching lowers stress levels and communicates affection in romantic relationships. Likewise, touch is linked to sympathy—just by stroking and patting our loved one. For a woman's psyche, for our soul or mind, the emotion of sympathy is a social practice, and we tend to display more sympathy than men.

Experts posit that touch in a relationship positively impacts psychological well-being—immediately and in the long run. This emotional regulation strategy builds social support and transmits responsiveness toward each other. At its core, the power of touch helps us regulate our emotions. By mutually touching each other, we develop a "touching culture" which contributes to our emotional well-being and couple synchrony. Affectionately touching our partner increases intimacy—we feel closer to our significant other. We display that we care about him or her— this nonverbal is easily decoded.

The overall quality of our relationship is stronger with the inclusion of partner touching. Both the physical and emotional states of each person are reinforced through touch. It brings a couple together through mutual feelings of being connected. It's also genuine and personal—or intimate—depending on certain touches. "The amount of accumulated received responsive touch in everyday life appears to have a long-lasting effect" (Debrot et al., 2013). By making an investment in your effective touch body language, you will reap benefits both immediately and in the future.

"Touch is a rich medium of social exchange and, through it, we form strong attachments and cooperative alliances" (Hertenstein and Keltner, 2010). Touch can also indicate "status differences, sooth and calm, and express sexual or romantic interest." When we are physically affectionate, we feel warm and secure with 'good' touches." When we love someone, a stroking touch may be exhibited to express our feelings.

Gender, touch, and emotion research (Hertenstein and Keltner, 2010) yields thought-provoking results. To illustrate:

1. Sympathy is communicated accurately through touch to the arm in couples in which one person is a *woman*. Think about who touches you and who you like to touch—and where do you touch these people?

2. Anger is accurately decoded when one person (of the couple) is *male*. I know you have strong feelings when it comes to arguing with *men*. How do you pick up on his emotions quickly? What do you see or know in your gut?

3. When we picture an angry person, the word "angry" defaults to a *male* face quickly. Are you thinking about his facial expressions or aggressive body posture when you see an angry *man*?

4. When we picture a happy person, the word "happy" defaults to an image of a *woman* first, not a *man*. I suggest you think about happiness and the images of who comes to mind.

5. Overall, *men* display more nonverbal aggressive behaviors than *women*. What nonverbals do you think are aggressive? No need to hear the words, as you sense the actions.

6. *Women* are better at accurately communicating happiness. Give some thought as to what words you use for happiness—Content? Thriving? Satisfied?

7. In general, *women* touch, smile, share emotions, and experience more prosocial emotions. Are you surprised that we touch, smile, and share more with others? Maybe not. Think about your relationships and the emotions you feel from each one.

"Men engage in more hand touches than women while dating but not during marriage," according to Smith et al. (2011), but other experts say that wives initiate touch more than husbands. In either case, touch has meaning. We touch for a variety of reasons, using our hands or bodies and display these touches in countless settings (in private or out in public) to demonstrate power, control, security, and confirmation of the relationship. "Romantic partners use touch as a strategy to get the partner to comply with a request," according to Smith et al. (2011). Sometimes we want our partner to cooperate, so we touch him or her—and it works.

Courtesy of Tiko Giorgadze

When we have an interest in someone, we express an immediacy pattern. We move closer, touch, gaze, lean forward, use greater facial expressions, and gesture more. A lot of these nonverbals confirm partner and potential partner interest. When we are physically close to our partner, this nonverbal cue triggers feelings of security while reducing threat. Positive rewards—like time and touch—have psychological and physiological payoffs. Touch simply improves our mood through caring gestures.

Additionally, closer partners often use softer vocal cues, gaze less, and are not necessarily facing each other as they communicate as they are already aware of the others expected nonverbal communications. Partners who have been together for a long time feel comfortable around each other and may spend long hours together without speaking or using intentional nonverbals. By this point, their body language is predictable and expected—the nature of the intimate relationship is well established. This increased "behavioral coordination" is perfectly timed between partner movements and is reciprocal.

How close do you like to get to your partner or a potential romantic interest? How do you touch each other? We build "behavioral synchronization" by matching certain nonverbal characteristics—this builds rapport between us. Known as the "chameleon effect" or "social glue," we subtly mimic our significant other to communicate and bond. Through mirror neurons in our brain, we recognize emotions, including the use of touch and space. We want to match our partner to feel connected—especially with our body language. Reflect on your romantic relationships, reach out and touch, and get close. Your brain—and heart—will thank you.

Fie, fie upon her!
There's language in her eye, her cheek, her lip,
Nay, her foot speaks; her wanton spirits look out
At every joint and motive of her body.

—William Shakespeare, *Troilus and Cressida*

CHAPTER 6

Influence is More than Impact

Be intentional with the type of nonverbal influence you want to display. Develop and maintain interpersonal relationships through social impact and live your passion through your actions.

"People will sever attachments with those whom they are incapable of influencing" (Bourgeois, Sommer, and Bruno, 2009). So, what does it mean to influence someone? Do you use intimidation? Do you encourage others through emotional appeals? Have you ever told a fib in order to get what you want? Sure. We're human. And our behaviors, without consciously thinking about it, impact our receivers—both positively and negatively. The impressions we make influence others, and our intentions—both nonverbal and verbal—drive behaviors and feelings.

We are constantly communicating in order to have our needs met and get what we want. Being able to successfully influence others helps us get there. Through informal, formal, and casual processes, and by being intentional, we convey information. Matsumoto, Frank, and Hwang (2013) offer three techniques to get what we want.

Technique	It's in the Details

1. Establish baseline behaviors.	A. Ask questions. Start with the easy to answer ones so you disarm him. Perhaps use "yes/no" questions.
	B. Watch his baseline behaviors. Perhaps clicking a pen, a touch to the face, tapping the foot, fidgeting with his glasses.
	C. Look for signs of stress/tension and physical body manipulations, called manipulators. These little unconscious fidgets offer comfort and help you pick up on his emotional state. Examples include:
	  1. Suddenly scratching the nose or face or somewhere on the upper body.
	  2. Clicking the pen and noting the pattern based on words, actions, and reactions.
	  3. Tapping or movement of the feet, if you can see them under the table or feel the table shaking.
	  4. When his legs are crossed, watch how the suspended leg moves up and down (swings).
	  5. Shifting in the seat or squirming in the chair. You are looking for movement.
	D. Listen to vocal cues—pitch changes, speed of talking, pauses, and swallowing changes.
	E. Try to match nonverbal actions and reactions with verbal clues for deeper understanding. Be aware of the differences as you continue the interaction.
	F. Bring a colleague with you, if possible, to observe him or other people in the room.

2. Establish what a hard "no" looks and sounds like.	A. Continue to ask questions. Watch what he says, how he says it, and what his body says (movement changes). B. You are trying to figure out a definitive "no" versus a soft "no." With a soft "no," hesitancy or subtle shifts in nonverbals happen and you "see" what he is really thinking. Internal thoughts are displayed through external behaviors.

(continued on next page)

Technique	It's in the Details
3. Focus on the crunch points to identify behavioral or verbal contradictions.	A. Concentrate on him. B. Listen and watch during the critical points of exchanging information. C. Watch for reactions in his body as you ask precise questions using particular word choices. Refer to the list above.

These body "leaks" also help us read the other person. Observation is crucial. There are nonverbal actions when looking at the other person, particularly during crunch times as mentioned in technique three. Observable body language includes:

Shaking the head to indicate "yes."'
Raising the eyebrows prior to saying "no."
Shoulder shrugging as if to say, "I don't know."
Showing open palm gestures to imply "I don't know."
Drooping the shoulders or exhaling to indicate relief.
Relaxing the torso and dropping the head to suggest defeat.

Courtesy of Raychan

Regardless of the situation or person, remember that it's important to manage your own behaviors. As you size up others, they are checking you out as well. Matsumoto, Frank, and Hwang (2013) point out, "The concept of managing your own behaviors and emotions is an important part of the process. . . . Just remember that the ability to emote is innate, and most people interpret our reactions at least on a subconscious level. You'll want to minimize your own information leakage. The secret [is] . . . to practice and plan in advance." Basically, be prepared and intentional.

HERE A LITTLE, THERE A LITTLE

We frequently influence each other and can make this influence intentional through controlling our particular actions. The following chart (Patterson, 2017) describes types (techniques) we use to exercise influence others using nonverbal cues:

Type of Nonverbal Influence	Meaning	Nonverbal Examples
Power & Dominance	• Control of self, others, and environment. • Often seen with powerful people.	• Physically close. • High levels of gazing. • Touching. • Usually physically relaxed (posture) when around subordinates or perceived lower-status individuals.
Feedback & Reinforcement	• Strengthens a desired behavior so it'll be repeated in the future. • Has the ability to influence—often more than words.	• Smiling. • Patting on the back. • Head nodding.
Compliance & Persuasion	• Used during both stressful and casual situations. • May increase compliance when stress heightens (eager to revolve conflict) or casually influence during low-importance situations. • Persuasion aims to change attitudes.	• Physically close. • High levels of gazing. • Touching.

(continued on next page)

Type of Nonverbal Influence	Meaning	Nonverbal Examples
Deception	• Discrepancies in one's words and actions. • Lying. • Struggle to judge a situation—may involve higher cognitive attention (need to think about what's happening).	• Slips in facial expressions or gestures when failing to align with words. • Inconsistencies in sending messages to receivers. • Changes in skin color—flushing, sweating, and blanching. • Hands shifting to face. • Change in tonal expressions (pauses, volume, word structure, speech rate, etc.).

The situation and the person are factors for which type of nonverbal influence we will use. Regardless, though, we have the endgame in mind when we engage. Specifically, two overarching goals result when we influence others:

1. A desire for control.
2. The perception that our life is meaningful.

We seek to have influence for a myriad of reasons—one being social acceptance or effect. Social influence, defined as "one's thoughts, feelings, or behaviors being altered by the real, imagined, or implied presence of others" (Bourgeois, Sommer, and Bruno, 2009), helps us to meet our goals. I encourage you to reread that definition. Note that communication and influence can be "real, imagined, or implied." No wonder we struggle to effectively communicate, influence, build, and sustain relationships! Perhaps the "it's all in your head" phrase applies to the potency of social influence.

There are also psychological benefits to having influence in creating and maintaining social relationships. As well, most of us enjoy having influence over others for several reasons.

Courtesy of Mariya Georgieva

Accuracy
Who doesn't like to be right?
We want to be correct and if we can get others to act and think like us, then we are justified that our actions and thoughts are right.

Belongingness
Don't we all wish to "belong" to something or someone?
When we connect with someone, we fulfill our "need to belong" with frequent interactions. When others approve of us, we may cave to the pressures or change our behaviors. With relationships, we have a sense of cohesiveness. In groups, we may make better decisions because we are on the same team.

Self-worth
Do you see your own worth?
When we influence another person, we gain a sense of accomplishment and are validated by the other person. We may even feel a sense of perceived competence because we are socially validated. No

doubt, the persuasive person feels confident that he or she has the respect and approval so desired and feels accepted by others.

Control
How do you navigate your life?
We must control our environment for our well-being and "control is enhanced by having influence over another's thoughts, feelings, and behaviors" (Bourgeois, Sommer, and Bruno, 2009). The mindset is that, when we influence others, we have a sense of control over our own social life—and, perhaps, others' lives, too. This is called "a power trip" if it is not controlled. If we use dominance, coercion, or force, this undermines our relationships. A feeling of control, however, is still extremely desirable.

Meaningful Existence
Do you have a purpose?
When we fulfill our goals, we feel a sense of achievement. By meeting our goals, we believe that our actions and ideas have value. We may do this through contributing something with lasting value.

These five benefits for seeking influence are not independent and may overlap when we are in the process of getting what we want. However, when we fail to have influence, our thoughts and actions may be negatively affected. As children, we call this a temper tantrum. But as adults, it doesn't look good to stomp your feet and lie on the ground screaming in frustration! Rather, we sulk, withdraw, or complain. Think about your relationships—how do you behave? Sometimes, it's not pretty, but we've all done it and witnessed it.

Assertions of dominance are often seen when we communicate and are important in understanding the dynamics of social interactions. We often communicate to get something we want; therefore, we overtly or covertly "dominate" through our actions and words. What dominance "looks like" is constantly being studied and is interpreted differently based on a host of accompanying nonverbal cues and situations.

When others fail to respond to us, we grow frustrated and stressed. We even become nonverbally unresponsive or put on a "poker-face." Even in infancy, babies will turn to self-soothing behaviors like thumb-sucking and looking away when their smiles and cooing aren't reciprocated. As adolescents, research confirms that parental rejection leads to negative attention-seeking behaviors in school, which "may reflect an attempt to regain a sense of control and attention." As adults, we will avert our gaze, physically retreat (step back), and soothe our bodies through self-touching behaviors like arm rubbing, arm crossing, or rocking back and forth.

As leaders, when we allow ourselves to be influenced by our followers, we are perceived as more competent and loyal. In turn, followers feel welcome, are more responsive, and are more apt to give their leaders latitude in decision making. We feel valued and respected with this exchange. When this doesn't happen, we can experience feelings of depression, anxiety, and withdrawal.

As we discussed in Chapter 4, when we mimic others' behaviors like postures, touching, and leg crossing, we develop stronger, positive feelings toward the other person. This "affect matching" is typically not conscious but influences us on a subconscious level. It's like the "monkey-see, monkey-do" saying—it doesn't require verbal language to understand. There is a positive relationship between non-manipulating nonverbals and influencing interpersonal interactions.

We want to be a part of a group—especially with others who agree with us. Evidence suggests that we feel discontentment when group members disagree, ostracize each other, and face leadership challenges. If our group is frequently in turmoil, we will most likely leave the group or not participate. The people in this questionable group no longer influence our thoughts and ideas. This is like having a bunch of arguments with your close group of friends. It gets old. You get tired of it. And, after a while, you withdraw following unsuccessful attempts to influence others. You basically grow weary of trying.

Depending on the situation, we use specific styles of social influence to get our way.

Social Influence Style	What This Means	Why We Use This To Get What We Want
Persuasion	A change in our attitude or belief—a result of receiving a message.	When we persuade someone, we feel right and have a sense of meaning. It bolsters our beliefs.
Conformity	A behavior change—matches the actions or responses of someone else.	When we conform, we may feel a sense of harmony or peace. We fit in with the group or agree with the influencer.
Behavior mimicry	Conforming to nonverbal behaviors—usually at an unconscious level.	We when mimic, we physically react or act like the other person, which enhances belongingness, self-esteem, and a feeling of being right.
Compliance	A behavior change—as a result of a direct request.	When we comply, we usually respond to someone's request and voluntarily agree. Sometimes aligned with control and/or belongingness.
Obedience	A behavior change—in response to a directive from an authority figure.	When we obey, we typically bend due to the hierarchical relationship or status. This feels like control.

Which social influence style do you tend to use to get what you want? Who do you want to influence? Sometimes we are intentional and direct with our actions toward a specific person or group. We'll even use intimidation, pressure, or imitation. At times, the other person will cave—or concede. And at other times, unintended consequences can happen. I encourage you to ask yourselves these questions:

What type of social influence do I like to use?
Are others aware of what's happening?
What is my intention?

Influence can be intentional or unintentional—it's important to keep this in mind as you consciously use nonverbal and verbal messaging to get what you want or need. However, nonverbal mimicry is usually unintentional. Much of it just happens when we interact with others. And, when used well, leads to a stronger sense of belonging. On the other side, we feel a greater loss when we try to influence our in-group, compared to out-group people, and fail.

Sometimes we try to persuade or influence through pressure—also known as peer pressure. We actually use various styles of social influence when applying pressure, except for behavior mimicry. With this coercive nonverbal style, there is little perceived pressure to change unless the nonverbal is physically threatening. For example, a glare that bores through your soul, or a little nod of the head confirming disappointment with a smirk on the mouth. These subtle, negative nonverbals carry strong influential messages and are easy to decode.

Keep in mind that due to our internal need for control and satisfaction, our self-esteem is innately tied to our level of influence on others. We gauge our needs and our various psychological demands to determine which can fulfilled by having influence. But, let's face it, who doesn't want to be influential to at least one person in his or her life?

PEARLY WHITES

Smiling disarms people. In general, we seek out smiles and mimic them in return. It's a nonverbal cue which is universally understood and makes others (and us) feel at ease. Some studies argue that smiling decreases the perception of dominance, whereas others say that smiling at people shows that you have command of the room or situation. Head tilting, however, changes how we feel in predictable ways. If you want to appear superior, "spontaneously tilt [your] head downward—and observers will reliably perceive this behavior as intimidating" (Witkower, Tracy, and Cheng, 2019). Think about it. This nonverbal action literally protects your neck and jugular vein, thereby keeping you safe from potential harm. Increase your eye contact (staring or glaring) and an awareness of your dominance, power, or control will emerge in yourself and others. On the other hand, a downward head tilt combined with downward eye gaze reliably (and cross-culturally) communicates "shame, submission, and low status" (Witkower, Tracy, and Cheng, 2019).

Prestige, an admiration or respect for another, includes feelings of warmth and likeability. Nonverbally, both the tilt of the head and smiling are seen to indicate prestige. Specifically, a slight tilting of the head increases interpersonal liking while conveying closeness and relatability. Emotions like happiness, excitement, and pride are associated with a prosocial upward head tilt. Combine this with a genuine smile, and we are perceived to be high ranking or important.

These nonverbals are important for connecting us with other people while also establishing credibility. A lot of positive feedback happens when we exhibit these nonverbals. I urge you to smile more, expand your body, and keep your head tilted upward—you'll just feel and look better while drawing others in.

When we display eagerness, open body gestures and hands projecting outward are common. When we lean forward toward the other person our eagerness is also easily observable. This approach-oriented nonverbal behavior boosts the effectiveness of our strategic influence. However, if our nonverbals do not match our verbal speech, our impact may be diminished or challenged. Smiling and active body gestures bring success in many situations, especially when we want to influence or sell another person on an issue or idea. We should also nod our heads "yes" to influence and persuade the other person (listener). Nodding is often viewed as an appeal to someone. Smiling also supports this.

By focusing on the physical aspects of a person, we may be distracted from what else is happening during an encounter. This can be intentional or subconscious. Our nonverbals "influence a message recipient's perceptions of communicator credibility, including a communicator's dominance and physical strength, clothing such as uniforms and white coats, reading glasses, hoodies, or other physical features such as facial laterality, baby-faces versus mature faces, facial hair, and tattoos," based on Guyer et al. (2019) studies.

Experts suggest that easy-to-process nonverbals automatically influence us because these simple cues do not require high-level cognitive thinking. Basically, we just react. There is a relationship between the amount of thinking, time, and confidence when we are processing nonverbals. We try hard to figure out the meaning of something displayed and how we'll react to it (how it influences us). Remember that "meaning is subjective" so one misused nonverbal can change an attitude—quickly!

How we receive others' nonverbal information has an impact on our attitudes. And often determines how we feel about their nonverbal displays. In turn, we react differently. When we lean in, smile, and make eye contact, we communicate positive "vibes" and our receiver's attitude will display interest and engagement. Without thinking about it, we gauge others nonverbals and are sensitive to negative nonverbal displays. If negative, we will naturally (and quickly) display similar nonverbals. Our in-group also influences us, as do the gender and race of those with whom we are communicating.

Courtesy of Priscilla Du Preez

Watching others' behaviors produces effects on the firings of neurons within our brains which then initiate us to behave similarly. These "mirror neurons" are automatic and fast. We will innately imitate or mimic others to "facilitate social interaction" (Guyer et al., 2019). This is one way to get the other person to do want we want.

We can also minimize avoidance by reducing resistance through persuasion. When we use open body positions, we are viewed as more persuasive. Animated, open movements while leaning in with fast body movements and speech are considered approach-oriented and welcoming. When we intentionally use nonverbals to support our verbal message, this "boosts the strategy's effectiveness" (Fennis and Stel, 2011). Via the social influence of obedience, we create a hierarchical relationship based on our status and how our prestige is perceived by others. Our nonverbals are important for status differentiation, including eye contact, body postures, and speech patterns (Zhang et al., 2019).

I recommend you learn how your unique personality traits "leak" from your body language. And I ask, how accurately can you self-assess? Self-accuracy is defined as the "ability to remember one's smiling, gazing, nodding, hand gestures, and self-touching during an interaction that has just occurred" (Hall et al., 2007). All too often we do (and say) something and then fail to realize how we actually looked "in the moment." We actually harm ourselves if our social interactions and relationships are not managed well. To add to this, often we are not aware that we imitate what other people do and express; it's an unconscious behavior.

Yet, if we fail to have a sense of self, or self-accuracy, we damage our nonverbal communication channel. For example, let's examine gender, influence, and self-accuracy. "Men are more likely than women to engage in emotional manipulation" (Grieve, March, and Van Doorn, 2018). Case in point, a man's negotiation skills are often better than a woman's skills because he's had a lot of practice. Due to women's strong links to emotional intelligence, research shows that women have greater interpersonal skills compared to men. Some even call us the "life of the party" as we mix, mingle, and "work" the room.

Since male roles are considered agentic and reflect power, dominance, and aggression, the ability for men to use or manipulate emotions may be tied to them having control. Women, on the other hand, are expected to be communal, nurturing, loving, and passive. The expectation of emotional manipulation does not default to her. However, for women who display less stereotypical communal roles, greater emotional manipulation is present. Some may resort to negative behaviors as a means of getting someone else to change, or worse, use deception as a means to cope and influence.

FIBBERS, FACTS, AND FALSEHOODS

Some people are just good at lying. While pathological liars primarily master the body language associated with deception, there are numerous small cues or clues to help us detect falsehoods, fibs, lies, and deception in ordinary individuals. Williams (2013) finds, when examining more than one hundred studies, that dilated pupils, fidgeting, and voice pitch changes are frequently used when lying. Gulabovska and Leeson (2014) posits that, when we see a variance between the face and the body, we show bias towards the body. Yes, your body language is talking!

Let's clarify deception and lying with clear definitions because we often use the two terms interchangeably and they are not the same (Matsumoto, Frank, and Hwang, 2013):

- **Deception** is "any action that misleads someone."
  1. May or may not be a deliberate act.

- **Lying** is "an act whereby someone deliberately misleads another without notifying that person that he or she will be misleading them."
  1. Is always a deliberate act.
  2. "Deliberate" and "without notifying" are important in a lie.

Of the two terms, we will focus on lying in that the person knows the information he or she is telling you is inaccurate and misleading. This person is a liar. And his or her lies are linked to his or her emotions. "The involuntary nature of emotions, along with their resultant facial expression and vocal tone means that lies will often 'leak' out in the nonverbal behavior—despite the liar's intention to conceal them" (Matsumoto, Frank, and Hwang, 2013). Both the face and the body get involved and usually the face and voice will confess the sender's intentions. "Without being able to see facial expressions, it is often hard to convey meaning and tone" (Brook and Servtka, 2016). Text messaging is a prime example of this! On the contrary, the body will express behavioral actions. The face will express emotions and the body will display physical actions like foot bouncing or postural shifting or freezing. What do you think she's thinking in this photo?

Trustworthiness and honesty are important social-moral characteristics and we "infer" levels of trust based on little information in a rather quick time frame. "Individuals rate trustworthiness as the 'most desirable' characteristic for an ideal person to possess," according to Brambilla et al. (2016) research. Their work connects dishonesty with low perceived partner similarities. In turn, both parties have "diminished behavioral synchrony." We just don't move together in sync when we question the other person's truthfulness. This is due in part to our disinterest in being associated with a dishonest person—so we won't act like him or her. We will be socially distant—even if we have to stand or sit close to the other person. On a moral level, "one may argue that coordinating our movements with those of a dishonest individual potentially leads to moral contamination" (Brambilla et al., 2016). Wow, moral contamination! I challenge you to figure out what's contaminating your life.

It is difficult to detect a lie. While we have our suspicions, actually proving that someone is lying can be exasperating. When lies are attached to emotions, the stakes are high. When there is a strong chance of a significant punishment if caught, or a big payoff for deceiving others, we call them "high stakes" lies. "Low stakes" lies, on the other hand, involve minimal risk, do not have emotional ties, and getting caught has little or no consequences for the liar. And let's face it, we've all told a "little white lie" and not been caught. Remember to exercise caution though. Lying is a complicated activity with no clear-cut answers with no single definitive nonverbal cue.

Detecting lies is not a simple process and the average person has about a 54 percent chance of catching deception (Bond and DePaulo, 2006). Basically, detecting liars is like guessing the result of flipping a coin. However, this may not be the case when it comes to deception and gender. Because women are able to more accurately decode nonverbal behaviors than men, some posit that women are better lie detectors—as well as more apt to lie. Others hypothesize that we are not able to identify deception of our own gender due to gender biases and preferences. We inadvertently miss cues of our own genders. Evidence supports the hypothesis that women outperform men on interpersonal sensitivity tasks like decoding others' nonverbals. This is backed by women's reputation of being more emotional than men.

Lloyd et al. (2018) research from 400+ participants viewing videos of lying and truthful statements finds a litany of gender-based deception outcomes:

1. Participants are more sensitive towards women than men.
2. They judge men as more truthful than women.
3. Women are more emotionally expressive than men.
4. Women are more likely to be judged as lying than men.
5. Judges do not find equal gender bias effects.

Because women are better at reading body language and emotions and, apparently, are better at manipulation, lying might be part of our skill set as well. Pease (2004) concludes that "women are far better liars than men" and we also "tell more complicated lies."

Remember that no single gesture indicates deception; rather, it is better to analyze "clusters" of nonverbals that deviate from baseline behaviors. A cluster includes at least three different nonverbal gestures or cues. Pease (2004) details common gestures associated with lying and their meanings.

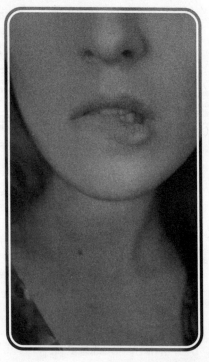

Courtesy of Azamat Zhanisov

The Nonverbal	The Meaning	Examples
Covering the mouth	Telling the brain to suppress deceitful words.	• A finger across the lips. • A fake cough. • Lips pressed together.
Touching the nose	Itchy chemicals (catechol-amines) irritate the nose; seen with increased blood pressure.	• Small stroke to the nose as if to scratch it. • Rubbing the nose area.
Rubbing the eye	Physically trying to shield the eyes from seeing some-thing or avoiding looking at the person who is being deceived.	• Men vigorously rub their eyes. • Women dab the areas below the eyes.
Clenching the teeth	Similar to covering the mouth, clenching the teeth "holds back" the lie from being uttered.	• Biting down on teeth or lips. • Chewing on the bottom lip. • Clenching the jaw hard so you can see the jawbone expand on the sides of the face.
Grabbing the ear	Blocking the ear as if to not hear the lie.	• Playing with an earring. • Covering the ear with the cup of the hand. • Gently holding the earlobe. • Bending the lobe to cover the earhole.
Scratching the neck	Signals uncertainty or doubt.	• Scratching the side of the neck below the earlobe—typically five times.
Pulling the collar	Increased blood pressure causes the vessels in the neck to swell and the neck to sweat. Attempting to cool the neck.	• Using the finger to pull the collar off the neck. • Fiddling with the tie.
Fingers or objects in or near the mouth	Self-soothing behavior lik-ened to reverting to suckling in infancy for security.	• Finger chewing. • Sucking on a pen. • Chewing gum. • Rubbing the mouth. • Playing with the mustache.

(continued on next page)

The Nonverbal	The Meaning	Examples
Swallowing hard	An attempt to suppress a lie. Can see the neck muscles while swallowing hard. The mouth might be dry or have extra saliva.	• Frequent swallowing when breaking from talking. • A cough or little choking sound. • Clearing the throat.
Changes on the skin	As blood pressure changes, our bodies heat and we ventilate through our skin.	• Sweating. • Flushing. • Blanching. • Patchiness on the skin.

We typically do not touch our hands to our faces. So, if you see someone change this baseline behavior and start moving their hands to their face and head area—something might be up. Touch also carries nonverbal significance in all types of relationships—friends, lovers, work associates, children, and even with strangers. We may touch someone to signal support or comfort, but touch also happens with aggressive body language. For example, a punch to the shoulder may be called horseplay in some instances, but assault in other situations.

Epstein's (1986) discussion of types of touch highlights that, frequently, touching indicates the nature of a relationship, as discussed in Chapter 5. In general, higher status (dominant) people initiate touch more often with lower status (subordinate) individuals. Epstein references this as a "pecking order." As you read this, no doubt you're thinking of someone who has touched you—and how you felt about it. Was it a work colleague? Your boss? Your best friend? A stranger at a bar? A man? A child? Or perhaps you initiated the touch. What were the circumstances? Were you seeking comfort or offering it? Were you indicating interest and how was it received? As we know, consequences from touch can be fruitful or damaging for both the sender and receiver. I urge you to be aware of this important nonverbal gesture.

When we glance away or avert our eyes, dishonesty, deceitfulness, and overall feelings of deception may be felt by the receivers of this nonverbal display. Glancing down may also indicate deception, according to Wilson (2009). Remember that deception and lying are different, and "avoidance by a good friend who keeps a distance and makes minimal eye contact is noticeable and uncomfortable" (Patterson, 2017). Deception is not always intentional, so be careful not to mislabel or jump to conclusions too fast.

In sum, the odds of spotting a liar are not good. Navarro (2008) states that even the most seasoned professionals like FBI agents and police officers have no better than a fifty-fifty chance at detecting deception. The most skilled or gifted are seldom right more than sixty percent of the time. It's important to understand the context of a situation, who's interacting as well as their influence, intentions, and the emotions involved. We know that emotions serve several purposes. Barrett (1993) states that they are "bidirectional, relational, significant processes" which have implications based on who is around us and our situations.

BELLY LAUGH

One way we seek to influence, build relationships, and resolve or manage conflict is through humor. It is "strongly associated with the formation and maintenance of interpersonal relationships" (Bippus, Dunbar, and Liu, 2012). This is a strategy for both non-verbal and verbal communication—particularly with conflict. We know that happy and satisfied couples use positive humor when things are going well—and less when there is discord.

"Partners use of affiliative humor in conflicts is associated with resolution of conflicts, feelings of closeness, and decreased stress" (Bippus, Dunbar, and Liu, 2012). The "trajectory of the interaction" is tied to humor, its specific use, and intent. Often, humor breaks the tension in a room and unites people. Or, if poorly timed, it can stifle a room and cause uneasiness.

Bippus, Dunbar, and Liu's (2012) research on the various types of humor specific to nonverbal displays and outcomes have important functions and observations for how we relate to each other. The chart below captures humor styles for close and/or romantic relationships.

Humor Style	Meaning	Why We Use Humor (Its Function)	How Others Rate Our Use of This Type	Related Nonverbal Observations
Affiliative	• Funny things to amuse others. • Facilitates relationships.	• Better for relation-ships than aggressive humor. • Seen as more intelligent, sincere, and friendly.	• Rated positively.	• Eye contact. • Gazing. • Open body posture. • Leaning in. • Hands visible. • Elevated vocal pitch.
Self-enhancing	• Coping mechanism. • Regulate emotions. • Keeps healthy perspective on negative situations.	• More effective than aggres-sive humor. • May be associat-ed with self-focused motives.	• Rated low credibility, likability, and apt to counter-argue.	• Unpredict-able eye contact. • Coy smiling. • Hands touching body.
Aggressive	• Sarcasm, teasing, put-downs, criticism.	• Makes the sender feel superior. • Mixed feelings of appreciation from others.	• Rated high for funni-ness and credibility. • Highest in counter-arguing.	• Glaring or staring. • Lower teeth displayed. • Mouth snarl. • Aggressive space con-sumption. • Loud vocal sounds.
Self-defeating	• Self-disparaging. • Amusing others at one's own expense.	• Seen as less confident, witty, and intelligent. • May be associat-ed with self-focused motives.	• Rated least funny.	• Head droop. • Eyes avert. • Body shift-ing. • Uneven mouth/lip movements. • Softer vocal sounds.

Regardless of the style, how we feel about humor impacts our relationships. When we don't agree on how the other person "comes across," we will focus heavily on the nonverbal cues we see—not the verbal words. This "verbal-nonverbal incongruence" mismatch confirms how important our body language is during relational interactions even when the situation is funny. Overall, men view humor more positively than women and will respond in agreement or disagreement more than women. We also tend to feel empathy towards the receiver of aggressive humor and will come to that person's defense, if necessary.

"A positive expression may trigger an empathic response," and we may even mimic the other person. Smiling, of course, adds to these positive feelings. However, the type of smile displayed will either kill the humor, upset your partner, or confirm positive responses. (Bippus, Dunbar, and Liu, 2012). There is a profound difference between a Duchenne smile and a smirk.

When messages contain humor, we are less likely to be critical. "Humor may be a wise communication choice in attempts to influence others," according to Bippus, Dunbar, and Liu (2012). But, as you know, the misuse of humor will make someone take you less seriously or evoke other emotions—like annoyance, disgust, or anger.

Even though women and men share similar feelings, emotions, beliefs, and nonverbal cues, there is no guarantee that humor will be sent and received the same way based on gender. There is some research that actually suggests that humor is received more positively by the opposite sex versus same sex individuals. Regardless, the nonverbals that accompany humor "may affect people's ability to relate to the humorist, and thus their reactions" (Bippus, Dunbar, and Liu, 2012).

Women's nonverbals tend to include gazing, smiling, facial expressions, touching others, posturing, and use of personal space to convey nonverbal messages. Men do not gaze, smile, and touch as much—particularly when they are trying to assert their social status, role, and personality (Hall, Coats, and Smith-LeBeau, 2005). Those with higher status or defined roles tend to gaze or display longer eye contact regardless of gender. Higher status persons are also freer to use humor without consequences. When we add humor to the mix, the situation can become more convoluted. I'm sure we've all been in the room when someone has uttered a crude or inappropriate joke. The room oozes discomfort—you actually see people cringe and avert their eyes. It's an awkward moment—so much for humor.

When we gaze at another person, different meanings can be inferred—power, aggression, affiliation, or even nurturing expressions can be perceived. Sometimes we even play the "staring game." This starts in childhood as infants stare at their protectors and caregivers. "If you do not pay attention to the nonverbal behavior, there is a great chance that you are missing much of what is actually being communicated by the other person. Thus, while active listening is always good, active observation is also necessary" (Matsumoto, Frank, and Hwang, 2013). And, this requires watching . . . and watching . . .

Courtesy of Joseph Gonzalez

The relationship between nonverbal and verbal cues is interesting. Most people don't question that spoken language is important. Of course it is. Yet, the interplay between the nonverbal and verbal are worth mastering because, when in doubt or when we want to influence, we will default to the nonverbal over the spoken message. Matsumoto, Frank, and Hwang (2013) describe various ways in which nonverbals interact with verbal content. Specifically:

1. **Substitution**: We'll use nonverbals in place of verbal statements. *A simple nod replaces a verbal "yes." Pointing towards something is easier than describing the location with words.*

2. **Repetition**: Including a nonverbal cue while also talking ensures that our message is received. *Rubbing our eyes while saying that we are tired shows the receiver how we actually feel through repetitive actions.*

3. **Contradiction**: When nonverbals and verbals don't match, this negative activity triggers suspicion. *Telling someone you are "not nervous" but wringing your hands actually exposes your anxiety.*

4. **Complement**: Nonverbals that align with our verbals enrich and focus our message. *Downcast eyes, holding your head down, and slouched shoulders demonstrate word reinforcement like "I'm not in a good place."*

5. **Accentuating**: A nonverbal that emphasizes certain spoken words. *Tapping fingers on the table while verbally scolding someone reinforces "why you're in trouble." One tap for every word spoken to accentuate the point. "You." Tap. "Cannot." Tap. "Go." Tap.*

6. **Regulator**: Unspoken actions help us organize and align conversations. *Walking around a room to engage people and hold their attention while verbally delivering the message.*

We communicate through our nonverbal body language to influence and navigate our world. We form impressions, judge behaviors, and develop strong positive or negative feelings about someone based on hundreds of unspoken communication cues. Sadly, the research also finds that "both sexes prefer humor that targets women" (Bippus, Dunbar, and Liu, 2012). And men will most likely have the advantage when using humor with their partner. Men also "rate humor, teasing more and are more likely to react with humor in anger-eliciting events."

YOU GO, GIRL . . . AND BOY

Gender impacts our ability to influence others. Several theories including role congruity, expectation states, and biosocial, affirm that men, more so than women, attain influence—both nonverbally and verbally—through perceived competence, assertiveness, and dominance. The variance in our pitch, as it is related to our nonverbals, also increases perceived or real beliefs about our competence. Studies suggest that pitch variation signals physical dominance—which is aligned with men. For example, if we hear a person with a trembling voice, we question their competence. And instinctively, we probably think of a woman's quivering voice. These "task cues" influence how others perceive us. We quickly pick up on a nervous speaker when he or she "um's," pauses, and jumbles his or her words.

These small, yet powerful, nonverbals can harm or help our ability to influence. Experts posit that men like when a woman uses strong task cues—like speaking firmly—as long as she is in a high performance role. When a woman uses tentative language or even somewhat pleading speech to influence, this reinforces her communal (friendly and warm) nature. As a result, men are influenced by it. For the most part, men do not like when women are agentic (domineering and aggressive). These behaviors can undermine a woman's ability to influence. I urge you to thoroughly understand our gender-driven communal and agentic expectations to influence others.

Courtesy of Eloise Ambursley

Two types of nonverbal signals are also aligned with influence—"dominant acts" and "deferent acts." Dominant acts are nonverbals which, literally, intend to dominate—like staring, standing erect, physical closeness, and pointing. Whereas deferent acts signal the intent to submit—perhaps through lack of eye contact, stooping posture, physical withdrawal, and closed or hidden hand movements. When we use dominant acts, we can induce stress in the other person. Men also use low pitch variation to dominate because testosterone is "positively associated with physical aggression" (Zhang et al., 2019). Men, then, are perceived to display dominant cues, win dominance contests, and be seen as influential.

There is a fine balance between agentic and communal qualities used to influence others. Women are penalized more when crossing these expected behavior boundaries. Generally, women have less status and power than men in many environments (Carli, 2001). "People assume that men are more competent and knowledgeable than women, that women are warmer and more communal than men, that men have more right to act as authorities than women, and that women must communicate communal motivation more than men." This is evidenced in both childhood and adulthood. In group settings, the default perception of influence goes to men and has a greater effect on group decisions. Back in the day, this spurred the idea of "the man of the house."

Gender dynamic outcomes suggest that men resist female influence more than women resist male influence. Men may resist a woman's influence as a way to maintain the power advantage over women. Even in childhood, boys influence both boys and girls; yet, girls are less effective in influencing boys. In the parental role, boys will heed to their father's requests more than requests from their mothers (Carli, 2001).

Courtesy of Ethan Hu

When a man interacts within a group of women, he will "exert a disproportionately large amount of influence" over the group's decisions—women tend to not do this. For a woman in a group of men, she reduces her influential actions. But, within mixed gender groups, women will exert "higher amounts of influence." The rationale is that the presence of other women empowers women (and girls) and urges them to participate. Men in these mixed gender groups will also show more support and agreeableness. We tend to serve as allies for each other. Think about girls and the study of science. Girls are not innately worse than boys. Yet, the numbers in professional scientific fields are not equal. As one Georgia science educator shared in Forbes (June 9, 2019),

> So many adolescent girls try so hard to fit in that they place their need to belong far above their need to pursue their interests. In class, many girls will answer questions but in small groups, and especially groups with boys, they look around to their peers before answering or proposing ideas demonstrating how unsure they are of how to express their thoughts and ideas. Science is (and should be) a process of learning to be wrong and then improving upon the mistakes. But, how could girls be wrong and still feel accepted? Many would rather just not speak up or participate at all to avoid the failure.

A man may find a competent and assertive woman threatening to his traditional assertive (agentic) role. Men report that they find highly competent women more threatening and less likeable than less competent women. These negative feelings adversely impact women's influence. Even when we exert the same amount of competent behaviors as men, men still do not like it. We have a disadvantage. Interestingly, though, when men believe there is an opportunity to gain money or other benefits, they are influenced to a greater degree by competent women. Money talks too! If there's something to be gained, a man's feelings of threat are overridden by his need for competence. Like everyone else, he wants his needs met.

Remember that those with high status assignments are more able to display nonverbal dominant cues like pointing, loud voice tone, and stern facial expressions when compared to low status people. And men are permitted to display these more than women in social situations. Nonverbal dominance is more acceptable from men—through strong eye contact, he gains status and authority. For women, this same behavior may result in being viewed as less likeable. Regrettably, competence is taken for granted in men; women usually have to prove themselves.

With our partners, if dominant nonverbals are displayed by them during a disagreement, it will be a challenge to persuade them to agree with our side. Keep in mind that men and women fail to influence when disagreements are backed by dominant nonverbals. The low status person in the relationship is truly disadvantaged when she or he displays dominant nonverbals. For example, we've all heard of a woman beaten by her husband for failing to "listen to him and do what he wanted." She "got in his face" and paid the price. His ability to influence her was challenged—but, she has the scars. Interestingly, both men and women do not like when a woman disagrees with them and they are less likely to be influenced or persuaded. I urge you to recognize these two unspoken sets of rules. Use your wherewithal to proactively influence—make a difference; be the difference.

Take advantage of the fact that when we are communal, we have great influence and power. We need to always remember that we influence through our body language as well as through our competent brains. If we don't use these influential nonverbal displays, then many naturally think we are self-centered. In groups, we are expected to be communal. If you apply this knowledge to your benefit, then we'll have influence.

Communality facilitates likeability, and both men and women benefit from this. However, the idea of "warmth" still defaults to women. In other words, even if a man isn't liked, he still influences. However, we are subject to the double standard that we must be likeable in order to influence. Yes, it is unfair. Yet, and fortunately, mindsets are shifting as more women lead and participate in groups—both social and professional. Hence, as we move to strengthen our relationships, gain control, and display warmth and competence, we must harness ourselves to get across the influential finish line. The power and intentionality of body language ensures that women will continue to influence and impact our world.

Getty Images

There's no way to know how many people your life will influence. You don't know who is watching, listening, or learning from you.

—Charles Stanley

PONDERINGS

You've made it! Yet, I believe there's more for you. I challenge you to ponder, reflect, and think about what stuck with you in this book. Below, I pose some questions and topics for you to consider. You may seek to make them a part of your world. What works for you? How can you make this change in yourself? What do you want to improve? These are just a few questions as you ponder the power of body language and how to be your best self.

CHAPTER ONE

Page 6   Which self-comforting action of "shielding, cleaning, or self-intimacy" do you tend to do when feeling uneasy? And how might you replace this action with a more empowering nonverbal?

_____

_____

_____

_____

_____

Page 13 Think about your body image. From the list, and specific to your shape/weight, how would you rate yourself? Critical? Upset? Ashamed? Guilty? Worrisome? Failing? What other positive or strength words could you use instead?

_____

_____

_____

_____

_____

Page 23 What is your favorite positive emotion and how do you display it? What emotion do you want to work on? List specific body language to reinforce this emotion.

_____

_____

_____

_____

Page 30 Watch your favorite TV show—but this time, watch the commercials and focus on the content. What gender, age, and racial stereotypes do you see? How do you feel when you see these images, and what do you think of the company's tactics for promoting these messages?

_____

_____

_____

_____

_____

CHAPTER TWO

Page 39 Think about someone you admire and someone you don't admire. Go through the five traits and answer "yes" or "no" about these two people. Now, think longer as to why you assigned these values to each person. What were you thinking or feeling?

_____

_____

_____

_____

Page 59   What's your favorite and least favorite body part? Do these align with your race? What do you think about the women surveyed all sharing the least favorite body part? Are you surprised? Now, list the actions you can take to change your negative feelings about your least favorite body parts.

_____

_____

_____

_____

Page 62   Looking at the list of triggers, which two do you relate to and display? What are the circumstances? How can you change this?

_____

_____

_____

_____

Chapter Three

Page 68   Look at the male and female nonverbals. Grab a friend and practice both gender actions. How do you feel when trying out body actions that feel uncomfortable?

_____

_____

_____

_____

Page 73 When looking at men or women, what are you "most attracted to" and why? And how does this impact your behavior towards these persons?

_____

_____

_____

_____

Page 80 From the 1969 *Glamour* quiz, how would you answer this today? What do you usually do when this happens?

_____

_____

_____

_____

_____

CHAPTER FOUR

Page 107 Which female are you in this photo? Past behavior or current? Is this who you want to be?

_____

_____

_____

Page 110 The friendship formula—do you agree with this? How much shared knowledge, experiences, and time have you invested in your close friendships? Are geography, family background, and racial similarity factors with your friend selections? Using your new knowledge from this book, how can you be a better friend?

_____

_____

_____

_____

_____

CHAPTER FIVE

Page 122   What's your favorite prosocial positive emotion? How do you display it?

_____
_____
_____
_____

Page 127   Are you a flirt? What's your style? Why do you do this? What's the payoff?

_____
_____
_____
_____

Page 137   Looking at this photo evokes thoughts and feelings from you. What do you feel? Are you guilty of bad facial expressions with your partner? How do you know?

_____
_____
_____
_____

CHAPTER SIX

Page 149   Spend ten minutes observing two or more people talking at work or during a social situation. What observable body language do you notice? Are you able to figure out various emotions—even without knowing the words? What parts of their bodies do they use or move the most? Facial expressions? Torso? Arms/Hands? Legs/Feet? Can you figure out if the interaction is going well or not?

_____

_____

_____

_____

Page 151   Reflect on reasons you want to have influence: Accuracy, Belongingness, Self-Worth, Control, and Meaningful Existence. Answer the related questions: Who doesn't like to be right? Don't we all wish to belong to something or someone? Do you see your own worth? How do you navigate your life? Do you have a purpose?

_____

_____

_____

_____

Page 163   What nonverbals do you typically see that confirm someone is telling you the truth?

_____

_____

_____

_____

Page 166   What is your humor style? What is your partner, friend, or coworker's humor style? What nonverbal actions confirm your answer? How does this style impact your relationship?

_____

_____

_____

_____

Bonus Ponder!

Page 175   Think about the "finish line." Where do you picture
           yourself compared to life's finish line? What's your
           social and professional influence? Are you where you
           want to be? How does your nonverbal communication
           confirm or deceive you?

_____

_____

_____

_____

_____

BIBLIOGRAPHY

Abell, L., Brewer, G., Qualter, P., Austin, E. (2016). Machiavellianism, emotional manipulation, and friendship functions in women's friendships. *Personality and Individual Differences*, 88 108-113. doi.org/10.1016/j.paid.2015.09.001.

Alleva, J. M., Martijn, C., Jansen, A., Nederkoorn, C. (2014). Body language: affecting body satisfaction by describing the body in functionality terms. *Psychology of Women Quarterly*, 38 (2), 181-196. doi: 10.1177/0361684313507897.

Axtell, R. E. (1998). *Gestures: the do's and taboos of body language around the world*. New York, NY: John Wiley & Sons.

Bahns, J. A., Crandall, C.S., Gillath, O., Wilmer, J. B. (2016). Nonverbal communication of similarity via the torso: it's in the bag. *Journal of Nonverbal Behavior*, 40, 15-170. doi: 10.1007/s10919-016-0227-y.

Balas, B., Kanwisher, N., Saxe, R. (2012). Thin-slice perception develops slowly. *Journal of Experimental Child Psychology*, 112, 257-264. doi: 10.1016/j.jecp.2012.01.002.

Balcetis, E., Cole, S., Chelberg, M. B., Alicke, M. (2013). Searching out the ideal: awareness of ideal body standards predicts lower global self-esteem in women. *Self and Identity* 12 (1), 99-113. Doi: 10.1080/15298868.2011.639549.

Barrett, K. C. (1993). The development of nonverbal communication of emotion: a functionalist perspective. *Journal of Nonverbal Behavior*, 17 (3), 145-169.

Becker, C. B., Verzijl, C. L., Kilpela, L. S., Wilfred, S. A., Stewart, T. (2017). Body image in adult women: associations with health behaviors, quality of life, and functional impairment. *Journal of Health Psychology* 1- 12. doi: 10.1177/1359105317710815.

Bello, R. S., Brandau-Brown, F. E., Zhang, S., Ragsdale, J. D. (2010). Verbal and nonverbal methods for expressing appreciation in friendships and romantic relationships: cross-cultural comparison. *International Journal of Intercultural Relations*, 34, 254-302. doi: 10.1016/j.ijintrel.2010.02.007.

Bippus, A. M., Dunbar, N. E., Liu, S. (2012). Humorous responses to interpersonal complaints: effects of humor style and nonverbal expression. *The Journal of Psychology*, 146 (4), 437-453. doi.org/10.1080/00223980.2011.652696.

Bond, C. F. J., DePaulo, B. M. (2006). Accuracy of deception judgments. *Personality and Social Psychology Review, 10*(3), 214-234.

Bourgeois, M. J., Sommer, K. L., Bruno, S. (2009). What do we get out of influencing others? *Social Influence*, 4 (2). Doi. org/10.1080/15534510802465360.

Brambilla, M., Sacchi, S., Menegatti, M., Moscatelli, S. (2016). Honesty and dishonesty don't move together: trait content information influences behavioral synchrony. *Journal of Nonverbal Behavior*, 40, 171-186. Doi: 10.1007/s10919-016-0229-9.

Brook, R., Servatka, M. (2016). The anticipatory effect of nonverbal communication. *Economics Letters* 144, 45-48. doi. org/10.1016/j.econlet.2016.04.033.

Bruder, M., Dosmukhambetova, D., Nerb, J., Manstead, A. S. R., (2012). Emotional signals in nonverbal interaction: dyadic facilitation and convergence in expressions, appraisals, and feelings. *Cognition & Emotion*, 26 (3), 480-502. doi.org/10.10 80/02699931.2011.645280.

Buil, J. M., Koot, H. M., van Lier, P. A. C. (2017). Sex differences and parallels in the development of externalizing behaviors in childhood: boys' and girls' susceptibility to social preference among peers. *European Journal of Developmental Psychology*, 16 (2), 167-182. doi: 10.1080/17405629.2017.1360178.

Bunnell, T., Yea, S., Peake, L., Skelton, T., Smith, M. (2012). Geographies of friendships. *Progress in Human Geography*, 36 (4), 490-507. doi:10.1177/0309132511426606.

Calogero, R. M., Pins, A. (2011). Body guilt: preliminary evidence for a further subjective experience of self-objectification. *Psychology of Women Quarterly*, 35, 428-440. doi. org/10.1177/0361684311408564.

Carli, L. L. (2001). Gender and social influence. *Journal of Social Issues*, 57 (4), 725-741.

Carney, D. R., Cuddy, A. J. M., Yap, A. J. (2010). Power posing: brief nonverbal displays affect neuroendocrine levels and risk tolerance. *Psychological Science*, 21(10), 1363-1368. doi:10.1177/0956797610383437.

Carton, J. S., Kessler, E. A., Pape, C. L. (1999) Nonverbal decoding skills and relationship well-being in adults. *Journal of Nonverbal Behavior*, 23 (1), 91-100.

Christakis, N. A., Fowler, J. J. (2014). Friendship and natural selection. *PNAS*, 111 (3) 10796-10801. Doi:/10.1073/pnas.1400825111.

Cialdini, R.B. (2007). *Influence: the psychology of persuasion*. York, NY: Harper Collins Publishers.

Costa, M., Dinsbach, W., Manstead, A. S. R., Bitti, P. E. R. (2001). Social presence, embarrassment, and nonverbal behavior. *Journal of Nonverbal Behavior*, 25 (4), 225-240.

Crane, E. A., Gross, M. M. (2013). Effort-shape characteristics of emotion-related body movement. *Journal of Nonverbal Behavior*, 37, 91-105. doi:10.1007/s10919-013-0144-2.

Dargue, N., Sweller, N. (2018). Not all gestures are created equal: the effects of typical and atypical iconic gestures on narrative comprehension. *Journal of Nonverbal Behavior*, 42, 327-345. Doi:.org/10.1007/s10919-018-0278-3.

Davies, K., Tropp, L. R., Aron, A., Pettigrew, T. F., Wright, S. C. (2011). Cross-group friendships and intergroup attitudes: a meta-analytic review. *Personality and Social Psychology Review*, 15 (34) 332-351. doi: 10.1177/1088868311411103.

Di Gennaro, K., Ritschel, C. (2019). Blurred lines: the relationship between catcalls and compliments. *Women's Studies International Forum*, 75, 1- 9. doi.org/10.1016/j.wsif.2019.102239.

Duan, J., Xia, X., Van Swol, L. M. (2018). Emotions' influence on advice taking. *Computers in Human Behavior*, 79, 53-58. doi. org/10.1016/j.chb.2017.10.030.

Eggert, M. A. (2012). *Body Language for Business*. New York, NY: Skyhorse Publishing.

Epstein, C. F. (1986). Symbolic segregation: similarities and differences in the language and nonverbal communication of women and men. *Sociological Forum*, 1 (1), 27-49.

Fennis, B. M., Stel, M. (2011). The pantomime of persuasion: fit between nonverbal communication and influence strategies. *Journal of Experimental Social Psychology*, 47, 806- 810. doi:10.1016/j.jesp.2011.02.015.

Friedman, H. S. (2019), Introduction to the special issue on theory in nonverbal communication. *Journal of Nonverbal Behavior*, 43, 107-109, doi.org/10.1007/s10919-019-00299-x.

Gheorghita, N. (2012). The role of the nonverbal communication in interpersonal relations. *Procedia- Social and Behavioral Sciences*, 47, 552-556. doi: 10.1016/j.sbspro.2012.06.694.

Gillen, M. M, Lefkowitz, E. S. (2011). Body size perceptions in racially/ethnically diverse men and women: implications for body image and self-esteem. *North American Journal of Psychology*, 13 (3), 447-468.

Goh, J. X., Hall, J. A. (2015). Nonverbal and verbal expressions of men's sexism in mixed-gender interactions. *Sex Roles*, 72, 252-261. doi: 10.1007/s11199-015-0451-7.

Grieve, R., March, E., Van Doorn, G. (2018). Masculinity might be more toxic than we think: the influence of gender roles on trait emotional manipulation. *Personality and Individual Differences,* 138, 157-162. doi.org/10.1016/j.paid.2018.09.042.

Gulabovska, M., Leeson, P. (2014). Why are women better decoders of nonverbal language? *Gender Issues,* 31, 202-218. doi:10.1007/s12147-014-9127-9.

Hall, J. A. (2006). Nonverbal behavior, status, and gender: how do we understand their relations? *Psychology of Women Quarterly.* 30, 384-391.

Hall, J. A., Coats, E. J., Smith-LeBeau, L. (2005). Nonverbal behavior and the vertical dimensions of social relations: a meta-analysis. *Psychological Bulletin,* 131 (6), 898-924. doi: 10.1037/0033-2909.131.6.898.

Hall, J. A., Mast, M. S. (2008). Are women always more inter-personally sensitive than men? Impact of goals and content domain. *Personality and Social Psychology,* 34 (1), 144-155. doi: 10.1177/0146167207309192.

Hall, J. A., Murphy, N. A., Mast, M. S., 2007). Nonverbal self-accuracy in interpersonal interaction. *Personality and Social Psychology,* 33 (12), 1675-1685. doi: 10.1177/0146167207307492.

Hall, J. A. Xing, C. (2015). The verbal and nonverbal correlates of the five flirting styles. *Journal of Nonverbal Behavior,* 39, 41-68. doi:10.1007/s10919-014-0199-8.

Hasson, U., Ghazanfar, A. A., Galatucci, B., Garrod, S., Keysers, C. (2012). Brain-to-brain coupling: a mechanism for creating and sharing a social world. *Trends in Cognitive Sciences,* 18 (2), 114-121. doi: 10.1016/j.tics.2011.12.007.

Hazem, N., Beaurenaut, M., George, N., Conty, L. (2018). Social contact enhances bodily self-awareness. *Scientific Reports,* 8 (4195), 1-10. Doi: 10.1038/s41598-018-22497-1.

Hess, U. (2016). Nonverbal communication. *Encyclopedia of Mental Health,* 3, 208-218. doi: 10.1016/8978-0-12-397045-9.00218-4.

Hostetter, A. B., Alibali, M. W. (2010). Language, gesture, action! A test of the gesture as simulated action framework. *Journal of Memory and Language*, 63, 245-257. doi:10.1016/j.jml.2010.04.003.

Jaegher, H. D., Di Paolo, E., Gallagher, S. (2010). Can social interaction constitute social cognition? *Trends in Cognitive Sciences*, 14 (10), 441-447. doi:10.1016/j.tics.2010.06.009.

Kana, R. K., Travers, B. G. (2012). Neural substances of interpreting actions and emotions form body postures. *Social Cognitive Affect. Neuroscience*, 7 (4), 446-456. doi: 10.1093/scan/nsr022.

Knofler, T., Imhof, M. (2007). Does sexual orientation have an impact on nonverbal behavior in interpersonal communication? *Journal of Nonverbal Behavior*, 31, 189-204. doi: 10.1007/s10909-007-0032-8.

Koppensteiner, M., Grammar, K. (2011). Body movements of male and female speakers and their influence on perceptions of personality. *Personality and Individual Differences*, 51, 743-747. doi: 10.1016/j.paid.2011.06.014.

Kuster, D., Krumhuber, E. G., Hess, U. (2019). You are what you wear: unless you moved—effects of attire and posture on person perception. *Journal of Nonverbal Behavior*, 43, 23-28. doi.org/10.1007/s10919-018-0286-3.

Lancaster, L. R. (2001, January). Girlfriend power Sisterspeak, *Ebony*, 28.

Latu, I. M., Mast, M. S., Bombari, D., Lammers, J., Hoyt, C. L. (2018) Empowering mimicry: female leader role models empower women in leadership tasks through body posture mimicry, *Sex Roles*, 80, 11-24. doi.org/10.1007/s11199-018-0911-y.

Lewandowski Jr., G. W., Mattingly, B. A., Pedreiro, A. (2014). Under pressure: the effects of stress on positive and negative relationship behaviors. *The Journal of Social Psychology*, 154 (5), 463-473. doi.org/10.1080/00224545.2014.933162.

Lloyd, E. P., Summers, K. M., Hugenberg, K., McConnell, A. R. (2018). Revisiting perceiver and target gender effects in deception detection, *Journal of Nonverbal Behavior*, 42, 427-440. Doi.org/10.1007/s10919-018-0283-6.

Mandal, F. B. (2014). Nonverbal communication on humans. *Journal of Human Behavior in the Social Environment,* 24 (4), 417-421. doi: 10.1060/10911359.2013.831288.

Marmaros, D., Sacerdote, B. (2006). How do friendships form? *The Quarterly Journal of Economics,* Feb, 79- 120.

Matsumoto, D., Frank, M. G., Hwang, H.S. (2013). *Nonverbal communications: science and applications.* Thousand Oaks, CA., SAGE Publications, Inc.

McDonough, P. (2009). *TV viewing among kids at an eight-year high.* Retrieved from http://blog.nielsen.com/nielsenwire/media_entertainment/tv-viewing-among-kids-at-an-eight-year-high/.

Men's Health (2019, January 2). Apparently, this is what the ideal male body type looks like. https://www.menshealth.com/uk/fitness/a758029/this-is-what-the-ideal-male-body-type-looks-like/.

Mills, J. S., Musto, S., Williams, L., Tiggermann, M. (2018). "Selfie" harm: effects on mood and body image in young women. *Body Image* 27, 86- 92. doi.org/10.1016/jbodyim.2018.08.007.

Modica, C. (2019). Facebook, body esteem, and body surveillance in adult women: the moderating role of self-compassion and appearance-contingent self-worth. *Body Image,* 29, 17-30. doi.org/10.1016/j.bodyim.2019.02.002.

Mongrain, M., Vettese, L. C. (2003). Conflict over emotional expression: implications for interpersonal communication. *PSPB,* 29 (4), 545-555. doi: 10.1177/0146167202250924.

Montiel, J. M., Bartholomeu, D., Flamenghi, Jr., G. A., Franco, F. G., Couto, G., Pessotto, F., Messias, J. C. C. (2007). Do first impressions count? Perceived nonverbal behaviors associated with social acceptance in university students. *Psychology,* 8, 1378-1389. doi.org/10.4236/psych.2017.89090.

Moya-Garofano, A., Moya, M. (2019). Body Image. Focusing on one's own appearance leads to body shame in women but not men: the mediating role of body surveillance and appearance-contingent self-worth. *Body Image*, 29, 58-64. doi. org/10.10/j.bodyim.2019.02.008.

Mucherah, W., Frazier, A. D. (2013). How deep is skin-deep? The relationship between skin color satisfaction, estimation of body image, and self-esteem among women of African descent. *Journal of Applied Social Psychology* 43, 1177- 1184. doi: 10.1111/jasp.12081.

Navarro, J. (2008). *What every body is saying: an ex-FBI agent's guide to speed-reading people.* New York, NY: Harper Collins Publishers.

Nelson, El. L. (2017). Here's why using the scarcity principle in your relationship will keep the passion alive. Retrieved from https://shesaid.com/scarcity-principle-passion/.

O'Leary, C. (2016). Catcalling as a "double edged sword": midwestern women, their experiences, and the implications of men's catcalling behaviors. *Theses and Dissertations* 535. Retrieved from https://ir.library.illinoisstate.edu/etd/535.

Overstreet, N. M., Quinn, D. M., Agocha, V. B. (2010). Beyond thinness: the influence of a curvaceous body ideal on body dissatisfaction in black and white women. *Sex Roles*, 63, 91- 103. Doi: 10.1007/s11199-010-9792-4.

Patterson, M. L. (2017). Nonverbal communication. *Neuroscience and Biobehavioral Psychology*, 1-10. doi.org/10.1016/8978-0-12-809324-5.06502-0.

Pease, A., Pease, B. (2014). *The definitive book of body language.* New York, NY: Random House, Inc.

Peker, M., Booth, R. W., Elke, A. (2016). Relationships among self-construal, gender, social dominance orientation, and interpersonal distance. *Journal of Applied Social Psychology*, 48, 494-505. doi: 10.1111/jasp.12529.

Proverbio, A. M., Omaghi, L., Gabaro, V. (2018). How face blurring affects body language processing of static gestures in women and men. *Social Cognitive and Affective Neuroscience*, 590-603. doi: 10.1093/scan/nsy033.

Rees-Miller, J. (2011). Compliments revisited: contemporary compliments and gender. *Journal of Pragmatics*, 43, 2673-2688. doi: 10.1016/j.pragma.2011.04.014.

Rowsell, H. C., Ciarrochi, J., Heaven, P. C. L., Deane, F. P. (2014). The role of emotion identification skill in the formation of male and female friendships: a longitudinal study. *Journal of Adolescence*, 37, 103-111. doi.org/10.1016/j.adolescience.2013.11.005.

Santos-Longhurst, A. (2018, August 21). How to tell when a man is stressed. *Healthline.*

Sell, A., Lukazsweski, A. W., Townsley, M. (2017). Cues of upper body strength account for most of the variance in men's bodily attractiveness. doi.org/10.1098/rspb.2017.1819.

Sauter, D. A. (2017). The nonverbal communication of positive emotions: an emotion family approach. *Emotion Review*, 9(3), 222-234. doi: 10.1177/1754073916667236.

Smith, J. C. S., Vogel, D. L., Madon, S., Edwards, S. R. (2011). The power of touch: nonverbal communication within married dyads. *The Counseling Psychologist*, 39 (5), 764-787. doi: 10.1177/0011000010385849.

Spangler, L. (1995). Gender-specific nonverbal communication: impact for speaker effectiveness. *Human Resource Development Quarterly*, 6 (4), 409-419.

Steele, C. M. (1997). A threat in the air: how stereotypes shape intellectual identity and performance. American Psychology, 52 (6), 613-629. doi:10.1037/0003-066x.52.6.613.

Steephen, J. E., Mehta, S. R. (2018). Do we expect women to look happier than they are? A test of gender-dependent perceptual correctio. *Perception*, 47(2), 232-235. doi: 10.1177/0301006617745240.

Stephens, D. L., Hill, R. P., Hanson, C. (1994). The beauty myth and female consumers: the controversial role of advertising. *The Journal of Consumer Affairs*, 28 (1), 137-153.

Tiggemann, M., Barbato, I. (2018). "You look great!": the effect of viewing appearance-related Instagram comments on women's body image. *Body Image,* 27, 61-66. doi.org/10.1016/j.bodyim.2018.08.000.

Watson, A., Murnen, S. K. (2019). Gender differences in responses to thin, athletic, and hyper-muscular idealized bodies. *Body Image*, 30, 1-9. doi.org/10.1016/j.bodyim.2019.03.010.

Watson, L. B., Lewis, J. A., Moody, A. T. (2019). A sociocultural examination of body language among Black women. *Body Image*, doi.org/10.1016/j.bodyim.2019.03.008.

Webster, J., Tiggemann, M. (2003). The relationship between women's body satisfaction and self-image across the life span: the role of cognitive control. *The Journal of Genetic Psychology*, 164 (2), 241- 252.

Williams, C. (2013, April 6). Lost in translation. *New Scientist*, 34-37.

Willis, J., Todorov, A. (2006). First impressions: making up your mind after a 100-ms exposure to a face. *Psychological Science*, 17 (7), 592-598.

Wilson, S. (2009). How to understand people: part 1: reading emotions: watch your (body) language: non-verbal cues play a significant part in communication. Sarah Wilson examines the meaning behind some of our most common gestures. *The Guardian*, 48, 1-3.

Winter, V. R., Danforth, L. K., Landor, A., Pevehouse-Pfeiffer, D., (2019). Toward an understanding of racial and ethnic diversity in body image among women. *National Association of Social Workers* 43 (2), 69- 80. doi:10.1093/swr/svy033.

Witkower, Z., Tracy, J. L., Cheng, J. T., Henrich, J. (2019), Two signals of social rank: prestige ad dominance are associated with distinct nonverbal displays. *Journal of Personality and Social Psychology*. 1-4. doi.org/10.1037/pspi0000181.supp.

Zhang. J., Reid, S. A., Gasiorek, J., Palomares, A. (2019). Voice pitch variation and status and status differentiation in mixed-sex dyads: a test of expectations states theory, role congruity theory, and the biosocial model. *Communication Research*, 46 (7), 986-1007. Doi: 10.1177/0093650215626976.

ACKNOWLEDGMENTS

First, to my family, who get a kick of out of watching me zone out as I research, create text, and polish my craft into the wee hours of the night. Without their unwavering support, nothing else would have mattered. Jerome, my fiance, thinks I am incredible—and, for that I am thankful. He's marvelous. My children, Evan, Jarrett, and Jillian, along with our Jenny and Courtney, are phenomenal human beings and added their images to this book with great zest. Hugs to you. And, for my mom, who trailblazed long before women received recognition for all of their accomplishments.

Second, this work would not be possible without the love, trust, support, and guidance of my pack of female friends. Shea's steadfast commitment to women's rights landed us at the Women's March in Washington, DC years ago and her drive makes me want to work harder—always. Janet's wisdom and humor make her a marvelous sounding board. To Christi, Daisy, Dana, Jayme, Jennifer, Karen, Kathy, Laura, Linda, Lori, Mary, Sharon, and Susie (in alphabetical order, of course!)—you are amazing women who make me a wealthy woman—I appreciate and value each and every one of you. From lunches to late night phone calls and sharing holidays and weekend time, you each encourage me because you are truly wonderful and generous women. Forgive me. I'm sure I missed someone who also makes my world special. I'll hug you in person.

Thanks to Robin Dreeke, for taking his time to read and craft a beautiful foreword from his perspective . . . knowing that in this busy world, he took his time to help me. And, I can't forget Joe Navarro who's just a phone call away. My editor, Elena Silverberg at Skyhorse Publishing, continues to assist me with moving important topics along and helping authors thrive. Any mistakes are mine in this book and I'll continue to make them as I plow through this world with only the intent to love, help, educate, and share. Remember, we're all in this together.